BIRDP~ ~R
GUIDE

RSPB

POCKET
BIRDFEEDER
GUIDE

Robert Burton

DORLING KINDERSLEY

LONDON, NEW YORK, MELBOURNE,
MUNICH, AND DELHI

Senior Editor Angeles Gavira
Senior Art Editor Ina Stradins
Editor Georgina Garner
DTP Designer Gemma Casajuana
Production Controller Bethan Blase

Managing Editor Liz Wheeler
Managing Art Editor Phil Ormerod
Category Publisher Jonathan Metcalf
Art Director Bryn Walls

This book contains material previously
published in *RSPB Birdfeeder Guide*
produced for Dorling Kindersley by cobalt id
The Stables, Wood Farm, Deopham Road,
Attleborough, Norfolk NR17 1AJ
www.cobaltid.co.uk

For cobalt id
Editors Marek Walisiewicz, Kati Dye
Art Editors Paul Reid, Darren Bland,
Pia Hietarinta, Lloyd Tilbury

Published by Dorling Kindersley Ltd
in association with the RSPB

First published in Great Britain in 2004
by Dorling Kindersley Limited
80 Strand, London WC2R 0RL
Copyright © 2004
Dorling Kindersley Limited, London
A Penguin company

Text copyright © 2004 Robert Burton
Additional text copyright © 2004
Peter Holden and Rob Hume

A CIP catalogue record for this book is
available from the British Library.

ISBN 1-4053-0250-X

Reproduced by Colourscan, Singapore
Printed and bound by
Star Standard Industries (Pte.) Ltd, Singapore

See our complete catalogue at
www.dk.com

Contents

Introduction

THERE ARE ABOUT 25 BIRDS that appear in gardens so regularly that they can be called "garden birds", but almost every species can be seen in a garden at some time or another. Observing, studying, and caring for these birds is a fascinating pastime and a significant industry, with more than 20,000 tonnes of bird seed sold annually in the UK alone. Gardens have become vital sanctuaries that help maintain the populations of birds under threat.

Observing birds in the garden is the best way to hone your identification skills.

Birds for all

Birds bring to the garden a fascinating diversity of colour, form, movement, and song, and watching their behaviour is the most immediate introduction to natural history for anyone – whatever their age.

Even pocket-sized city gardens are visited by a few species, and nearby parks provide many opportunities for both birds and birdwatchers. Suburban and country gardens support more diverse communities of birds, and are an important extension of habitat for birds that have found life increasingly tough in the

Birds visiting gardens *include rare birds of prey, such as the Red Kite (right), and old friends like the Blackbird (below). Watching, studying, and understanding the behaviour of common species is every bit as rewarding as the occasional glimpse of a rarity.*

countryside. Whatever the size of your garden, providing food, water, and shelter will always tempt more species to visit.

Some bird species thrive near human habitation, feeding and nesting in gardens. Others, which may be common in the countryside, rarely come near houses, or only enter the largest gardens with mature trees and shrubs. Others still may just pass through, perhaps swept off-course when on migration or driven by hunger to search for food. The predictability of old friends, the seasonal shifts of migrant populations, and the prospect of unexpected visitors makes the garden the best of all bird observatories. And by adding feeders, nest-boxes, and bird-baths, and planting bird-friendly plants, it can be transformed into a bird sanctuary that will provide wildlife interest all year round.

Garden successes

Many more birds now come into gardens than they did 20 years ago, and the variety of species seen has increased dramatically – a survey by the British Trust for Ornithology recorded a staggering 162 species of birds feeding in British gardens. Some of these species, notably the Siskin, Goldfinch, and Long-tailed Tit, have only recently become regular visitors. Siskins, for example, were once rather rare birds in the south of England, but in 1963 they started to come into gardens to feed on peanuts in plastic mesh bags, and now they are common winter visitors in many gardens around the country. New research is revealing new kinds of food that will lure even more species into gardens.

PAST PRACTICES

Historical documents show that people have been feeding and caring for wild birds for centuries. The poet Geoffrey Chaucer wrote of the "tame ruddock" (the ancient name for the Robin), which suggests that it was already a garden favourite in the 14th century. Burgeoning interest in wildlife and bird conservation in the late 19th century gave bird feeding an environmental perspective, and today its importance to the survival of wild bird populations is acknowledged.

By the 19th century, *putting out crumbs for Robins and other birds was an accepted pastime.*

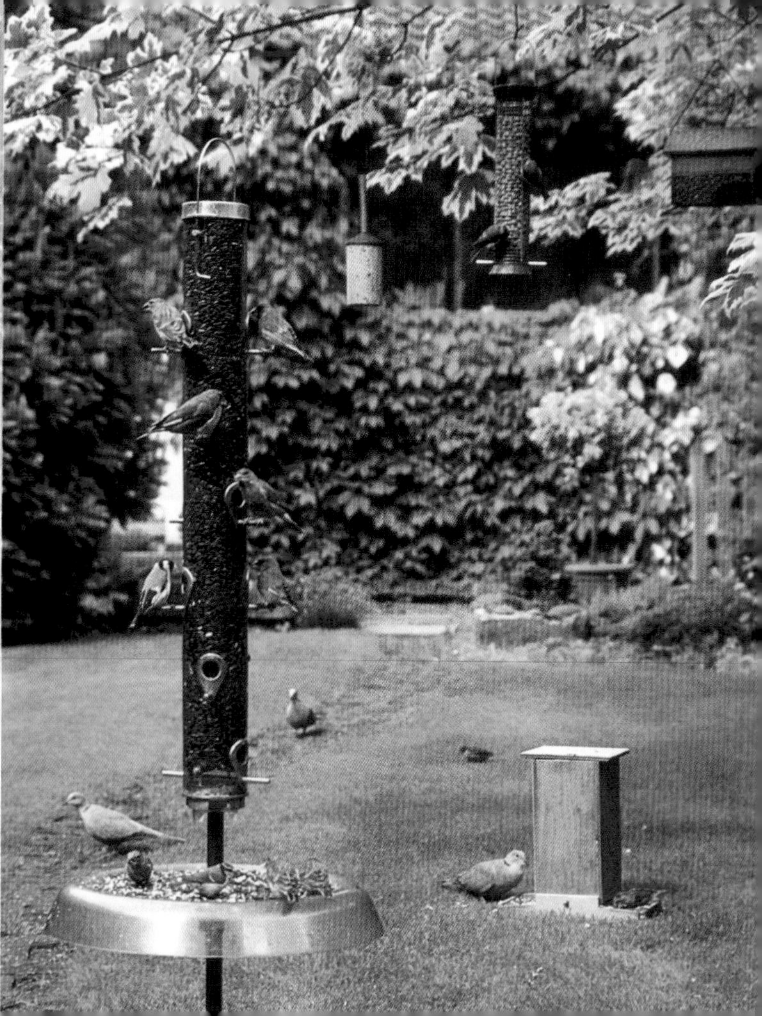

The diversity of birdfeeders available has quadrupled the number of species that visit European gardens over the past two decades.

Disappearing birds

Throughout Europe, the last 30 years have seen dramatic declines in numerous garden bird species – especially those which spend part of their lives in the open countryside. Rural House Sparrow and Song Thrush populations, for example, have plummeted by more than 60 per cent since the 1970s across much of Europe. Bullfinches and Tree Sparrows, as well as ground-nesting birds, such as the Skylark and Curlew have also followed downward trends.

Changes in European agricultural practices have profoundly affected bird numbers. Intensively farmed fields (left) have replaced traditional grazing meadows (above).

Threats in the wild

Explaining the decline of one species is never easy, because a combination of factors is usually involved. Some blame increasing numbers of predators and nest robbers, such as Sparrowhawks and Magpies, for falling songbird populations, but there is little evidence that these predators ever have more than a local effect. It is more likely that declines are linked to the degradation and disappearance of habitat. New buildings and roads have eaten away at the countryside, while changes in agricultural practices seriously affect feeding and breeding opportunities for birds.

The move to gardens

The intensification of agriculture has replaced a varied farmed landscape of fields, hedges, and rough corners with dense monocultures of crops. Fruitful hedgerow shrubs have been grubbed out, and pesticides and herbicides have removed the invertebrates and weeds on which many birds depend for food. Sixty years ago, a square metre of ordinary ground contained an average of 2,000 seeds; now an average square has just 200 seeds.

More efficient harvesting of cereal grain and better storage have depleted the amount of grain left on the ground for birds during the tough winter months. New varieties of cereal crops can be grown at such high densities that birds are unable to move between the plants to feed and nest. A particularly significant change to farming practices has been the move from spring-sown to autumn-sown cereal crops, resulting in the disappearance of stubble, which was once an important source of winter food.

With all these changes in the countryside, and the growth of birdfeeding as a hobby, it is no surprise that domestic gardens are becoming increasingly important as a source of food and a safe refuge for birds, particularly in the winter months.

The garden is a resource for enterprising birds, such as this nesting Spotted Flycatcher.

Plants – even those grown for their ornamental value – may be a food source for birds. Greenfinches (far left) visit sunflower seedheads, while House Sparrows (left) take nectar from red hot pokers.

When to feed

Birds benefit most from supplementary feeding at two times of year – towards the end of winter and during the nesting season. In winter, insects are scarce, and birds take seeds as the main part of their diet. When this resource runs out, birds flood into gardens in search of food. In years when hard frosts and snow lock up food supplies, some birds may starve to death. Lack of food makes others less alert, and so more likely to fall prey to predators.

Gardens are also often short of natural foods when birds are rearing their young. Summer feeding encourages birds into the garden, and these may stay faithful through the autumn. Greenfinches nest earlier in gardens if fed on sunflower seeds, and Blue Tit survival is improved if the birds can take a quick snack while searching for insect food for their nestlings.

Helping garden birds

Studies by ornithologists show that gardens are rather poor habitats for birds when compared to woodland and traditional farmland. With time and planning, however, it is possible to transform almost any garden into a haven for birds. This involves planting and landscaping the area in such a way that it provides natural sources of food for different birds throughout the year, and so that it contains suitable cover for roosting and nesting (see pages 42–47). A mixture of trees, shrubs, lawn, and herbaceous beds, for example, recreates a woodland glade habitat and provides food and shelter opportunities for a range of species.

Feeding

Creating a wildlife garden is an immensely rewarding project, but there are more immediate ways to attract birds into your garden. The simplest is to put out home-made or proprietary foods in your garden, using purpose-built bird-tables and feeders.

In the 1970s, kitchen scraps, half-coconuts, and strings of monkey nuts were the most popular foods left out for birds. In the 1980s, red plastic nets filled with shelled peanuts appeared in millions of gardens. However, the nets also proved convenient for squirrels, which could rip them open and steal their contents. These were replaced by purpose-built, tubular, metal-mesh and clear plastic feeders, which could be filled with food specially formulated for birds. Today's feeders are highly sophisticated, can be sited in almost any garden location (see page 21), and are designed to attract or exclude particular bird species.

NEW HABITATS

As the farmed countryside provides ever fewer opportunities for birds, the role of gardens as wildlife sanctuaries has increased. Britain alone has 270,000 hectares of private gardens and a further 150,000 hectares of parks. There are also large areas of roadside verges, "brownfield" sites, playing fields, cemeteries, and other open spaces which support birds.

A juvenile *Song Thrush faces an uncertain future. The species is in decline, and gardens with plenty of food are welcome sanctuaries.*

Wrens starve *because they cannot find food when the ground is covered with snow. Clearing the ground in sheltered places and putting out cheese can be a critical aid.*

What birds need

Success in attracting birds depends on how well you can provide for their basic needs. Even if your garden does not contain a natural wealth of food or large, mature trees, you can copy these features in the garden by providing food, birdfeeders, and nest-boxes.

The basics

MOST WILD ANIMALS ARE DEPENDENT on four major factors in their habitat – food, cover, water, and space. Even in the smallest rooftop garden it is possible to provide birds with food and water, while the average suburban garden can passably recreate the woodland favoured by most common bird species. Knowing their needs can help us boost the number of bird species that visit.

Water as well as food *is an important resource that you can provide.*

New habitats

Until about 7,000 years ago, much of Europe was covered in primeval woodland. Our Neolithic ancestors converted much of this to farmland, but even in the early Iron Age, about 2,500 years ago, about half of the continent was covered in forest. Since that time, a total transformation has taken place. Habitats have changed beyond recognition, and a new one – suburbia – has been created. It is in our suburban gardens that we have our closest contact with nature.

Even with our help, *life is tough for garden birds. Of a brood of Blue Tits, on average, only two will survive until the next spring.*

DAILY FOOD INTAKE

Daily food intake differs from species to species. The higher the calorific value of the food, the less the birds need to find. A Yellowhammer feeds on seeds that have a higher nutrition content than the slugs and snails favoured by Song Thrushes.

	Daily food requirement (per cent of body weight)						
	0	20	40	60	80	100	120
Heron	Fish						
Yellowhammer	Seed						
Blackbird	Earthworms						
Song Thrush	Slugs and snails						

The mixed forested landscape of our ancestors has become a blend of different habitats, most of which appear in microcosm – a clump of trees here, and a grassy clearing there. Some of the old forest residents have learned to thrive in this new habitat, while others need human assistance.

Food and drink

The easiest way to attract birds into the garden is to provide them with nutritious, energy-rich foods in the winter months. Food gives birds the energy to stay alive, and the colder the weather, the more they need. Small species lose heat quicker than larger ones and so have to feed more frequently. A Blue Tit, for example, spends 85 per cent of a winter's day searching for food, and a Blackbird will take over 300 berries a day from a pyracantha bush.

Feeding in the summer is also important, and a growing brood makes great demands on its parents. A pair of adult Blue Tits, for example, will gather as many as 1,000 caterpillars each day to feed to their young. Water, too, is essential, both for drinking and bathing;

Some birdfeeders are *designed so birds can take only the correct size food (left), thus avoiding any danger of choking. Others are enclosed in cages (above) to protect the food from bandits, such as squirrels.*

seed-eaters in particular need to drink plenty of water. Your garden may already contain a pond or stream, or even natural hollows at the bases of tree limbs that trap rain water. Adding water holes or bird-baths to the garden will attract all sorts of interesting wildlife, not least birds.

Safe places

All birds need cover from predators and protection from the elements, especially in the breeding season. Cover can be provided naturally by trees, shrubs, banks, hedgerows, or artificially, by nest-boxes. Thorny bushes make excellent protective thickets, and an old teapot upended in a tree or shrub makes a good nest site for a Robin. Leave a window open in your garden shed; birds are great opportunists, and a Blackbird or Song Thrush may well take this chance to raise its young out of the reach of cats.

This chapter contains a wealth of ideas to help you to transform your garden into a rich bird habitat that will bring you pleasure year-round.

NIGHT AND DAY
The amount of time a bird can spend feeding is limited by daylight, which varies greatly with the seasons, especially at northern latitudes. In winter, a bird may have just eight hours or less to feed; it converts its food to fat, and burns the fat reserves to survive the following hours of darkness. Small birds cannot store enough fat to last through more than one night.

Hanging birdfeeders

THE FOOD THAT MANY BIRDS NEED, especially in winter, often grows at the ends of slender branches and twigs: thousands of seeds make up birch catkins, for example, and alder seeds are hidden in small cones. Many small, agile species are well adapted to feed from this hanging harvest, and it is easy to tempt these attractive birds into the garden by putting up hanging birdfeeders. Different designs favour different species.

HANGING BIRDFEEDER BIRDS

Birds you are most likely to see on a hanging birdfeeder include:

- Blue Tit
- Great Tit
- Coal Tit
- Long-tailed Tit
- House Sparrow
- Great Spotted Woodpecker
- Starling
- Greenfinch
- Siskin

The specialists

The birds most likely to come to hanging birdfeeders are those most adapted to living high in trees or shrubs where they naturally cling to swinging twigs or hang upside down to grab food from under leaves. Blue and Great Tits are the most familiar visitors, but Coal Tits, and Siskins are also regulars. Surprisingly, Long-tailed Tits, which are well adapted to a hanging style of feeding,

Siskins feed by hanging from branches of birch or alder to take seeds, and so can easily adapt to feeding on hanging birdfeeders in your garden.

have only begun to take food from feeders in recent years. Among other birds, Nuthatches, which are often seen clambering jerkily up and down tree trunks, have also learned to visit garden feeders, as have Great Spotted Woodpeckers.

Feeders fitted with perches enable less agile species such as the Chaffinch and Goldfinch to feed alongside the accomplished acrobats. Hanging feeders are typically filled with peanuts, but using other foods (see page 26) helps to increase the variety of visiting species.

Learning the ropes

Hanging feeders will also attract species that do not normally eat suspended food. House Sparrows and Starlings have, for many years, copied the acrobatic tits and finches and learned to cling – usually rather

TYPES OF HANGING BIRDFEEDER

A large wire mesh feeder holds enough peanuts to last several days before refilling. It attracts species like the Nuthatch.

Mesh feeders are coated with zinc to prevent corrosion, and offer excellent protection against squirrel damage.

Log-style feeders blend into the garden landscape – ideal for gardeners who favour the natural look.

A simple wire basket filled with peanuts is sufficient to attract unusual birds, such as the Siskin, into the garden.

Peanut feeders are designed to ensure that parent birds cannot take whole nuts, which could choke their young.

clumsily — on to the feeders. Robins have also learned by observation: they will often hover, hummingbird-like, at a feeder, as they take dainty pecks at the hanging food.

Hanging birdfeeders can be a target for larger birds that have learned to exploit this ready-made food source. Jackdaws and other crows, for example, will sometimes raid feeders, while a Sparrowhawk may make occasional dashing raids into a garden to prey on unsuspecting birds that are using a hanging birdfeeder.

Exciting species, *such as this Great Spotted Woodpecker, can be seen at feeders throughout the year, but are most likely to visit in the winter.*

Warm fat *studded with seeds, set in a ceramic "bell", is particularly good for birds that feed upside down.*

This seed feeder *has an opening at the base that allows seeds to fill a shallow tray. A roof keeps the seed dry.*

Clear plastic tubes *can be filled with a mixture of seeds. Specially designed feeding ports allow access for birds.*

A seed tray *fitted to the base of a tube feeder catches spilt seed. Drainage holes ensure the seed remains dry.*

The multiple feeding *ports on this giant feeder have perches and are offset to maximize feeding access.*

Specialist birdfeeders

MOST BIRDFEEDERS are designed to attract the widest possible range of common species, though they tend to be visited mainly by tits and finches. As gardening for birds has become more popular, feeders have been developed that attract specific birds, or which deter certain birds or predators. A bird garden that draws in an interesting mix of visitors is likely to contain a variety of feeders.

Careful selection of food and feeders can attract species like the Linnet.

Unwanted visitors

Hanging feeders are an excellent means of delivering food to garden birds because they keep seeds or nuts beyond the reach of mice and rats. Grey Squirrels, however, are harder to exclude because they can climb the thinnest branches, jump gaps of 2m (6ft) or more, and chew their way into all but the most robust feeders. In many cases, they not only eat the food, but render the feeders unusable.

There are a number of squirrel deterrents available for garden feeders. These include plastic domed baffles with steep sides to prevent access, and wire cages around the container. The cages allow small birds to enter, while excluding squirrels and larger birds. Cages also give protection against Sparrowhawks –

Sparrowhawks soon discover the feeding places of their prey, and make bold attacks at garden birdfeeders.

BIRDFEEDERS AND ACCESSORIES

Window feeders attached with plastic suction caps give close-up views of birds, ideal for people who live in flats.

Wall-mounted peanut feeders are perfect for smaller gardens with no trees. They attract smaller species, such as Blue Tits.

Rings made from mixed seeds and melted fat can be hung from low branches to make an excellent high-calorie snack.

The "squirrel baffle" over this feeding station has a pivot, and tips to the side when a squirrel attempts to get a foothold.

Corrosion-proof poles can elevate a feeder if there are no trees in the garden, or help make the best use of limited space.

Grey squirrels are *highly resourceful and will exploit any food source. They have chisel-like front teeth and well-developed jaws which can cut through the wire of a hanging feeder.*

swift, agile predators that frequent the feeding haunts of small birds. Protective cages must be large enough to stop a squirrel reaching the food with its paws (Sparrowhawks too have a long reach); although squirrels have also been known to gnaw through supporting rope or wire and carry off entire feeders.

Feeding for diversity

Increasing the range of foods available in the garden will almost always attract a greater variety of birds. Specialized birdfeeders are designed to hold particular types of food: millet and nyjer seed, for example, are finer than most other bird foods; they need to be held in custom feeders with small port holes.

Steel bars *protect a polycarbonate feeder with metal feeding ports.*

Nyjer seed *is held in a feeder with small feeding ports. It is a favourite of Goldfinches, but also attracts Siskins.*

A guard *with a mesh size of about 5 x 5cm (2 x 2 in) allows small birds to feed, but excludes larger species and squirrels.*

Holders *for fat-based bird foods, such as this peanut cake, allow the cake to be hung from a branch or pole.*

Peanut cake *studded with seeds can be placed into a rustic, natural feeder, made from bent reeds tied with twine.*

A woodpecker *feeds at a peanut cake. Starlings can be discouraged by placing a CD over the top of the cake.*

Ground feeders

SUCCESS IN ATTRACTING a wide variety of birds to the garden depends on how well the natural feeding habits of different species are catered for. While many common garden birds readily adapt to hanging birdfeeders and bird-tables, others are much happier feeding at ground level. A well-planned bird garden needs to consider all the species that may visit and ensure there are the appropriate feeders to meet their needs.

GROUND FEEDER BIRDS

▦ Birds you are most likely to see on a ground feeder include:

- Collared Dove
- Pied Wagtail
- Dunnock
- Mistle Thrush
- Song Thrush
- Starling
- Chaffinch
- Greenfinch

Feeding on the ground

Some species, such as tits and finches, are adept at finding food in the slender branches of trees and shrubs and they readily adapt to feeding on hanging feeders and on bird-tables. Others, such as Robins and Starlings, have watched and imitated this behaviour. A number of species, however, including Dunnocks and Song Thrushes, visit gardens but mainly forage for food on the ground, only rarely venturing on to bird-tables, preferring those without roofs.

Food can, of course, be spread on the ground to make it available to all species. However, food lying on the ground can quickly be spoiled by wet or snowy weather, potentially causing hygiene problems, so it is best to provide food on low bird-tables (see page 24) or in ground feeders, such as hoppers.

Feeder variety

Many of the larger species that feed mainly on the ground tend to arrive in flocks, quickly snapping up any available food. Supplying the food in hoppers (see below) allows a controlled release of food, and also prevents seed from being blown away by strong winds. Caged hoppers, which restrict species by size, help to ensure that the smaller, shyer species get their fair share, and also give protection from predators, such as cats and squirrels.

The Song Thrush is at home feeding on the lawn. It will visit a bird-table, but it never visits hanging feeders.

TYPES OF GROUND FEEDER

This plastic hopper releases food from a lower tray as the birds eat. Prevent damage to the lawn by moving it every few days.

Plywood hoppers are simple and inexpensive. This hopper is easily dismantled so that it can be cleaned inside and out.

Caged hoppers allow small birds like Dunnocks to feed undisturbed, while larger species such as Woodpigeons are excluded.

Metal hoppers are sturdy and weather-resistant. The cage prevents large birds and squirrels from feeding.

SITING FEEDERS

To attract the maximum number of birds to the garden, it is best to have a variety of feeders in different locations. As a general rule, place hanging feeders near the house for less shy species and away from the house for those that are timid. Put ground feeders and low bird-tables on the lawn for those species that cannot normally be encouraged on to a bird-table or feeder. There is considerable overlap between species and the feeders they use, so the secret is to experiment with different feeders in different positions until all are being fully used. When choosing where to put feeders and tables, however, make sure that they are safely out of reach of predators, such as cats.

Positioning *a bird-table close to the house will give you a good view. Blackbirds are frequent visitors.*

The boldest birds, *such as the Blue Tit, visit window feeders, giving wonderful viewing opportunities.*

A caged hopper *is good for an open position. Small birds, like the Chaffinch, can see predators coming and are afforded some protection.*

A hanging peanut *feeder, sited close to cover, will attract regular visitors, like the Siskin.*

Starlings *visit birdfeeders and tables to feed. Hanging feeders from the edge of a bird-table is a simple way of providing both options.*

Pole-mounted feeders *can be moved around the garden to find the most popular spot. They attract birds like House Sparrows that feed on seeds and peanuts.*

Tubular feeders *attract acrobatic visitors, such as Coal Tits. When siting a feeder in a tree, be sure there are no overhanging branches that allow easy access to cats and squirrels.*

Greenfinches *often visit birdfeeders in small flocks, and so make good use of larger tubular feeders attached to trees.*

A well-stocked *low bird-table will attract ground-feeding birds, such as the Song Thrush.*

Birds that *do not usually feed on bird-tables, like the Collared Dove, may venture on to a hanging table just above the ground.*

Making feeders

As the popularity of feeding birds in the garden grows, so more feeding equipment becomes commercially available. It is, however, relatively easy to make some basic feeders at home using commonplace materials. The results may be just as successful, at considerably less expense, and the rustic look of home-made feeders blends well with the garden environment.

Simple feeders

There are many simple methods of feeding garden birds that do not involve expensive equipment or complicated construction. A coconut sawn in half and suspended on string, for example, is very attractive to Blue and Great Tits, while hanging peanuts in their shells also attracts the same species. Bones from cooked meat suspended from trees and bushes will usually be pecked clean within a few days.

Fatty food is very valuable to birds as a winter supply of protein. A log can be smeared with cooked fat, or have large holes drilled in it into which suet or other fat can be pressed (see below). This is enjoyed not only by tits, but also Nuthatches and woodpeckers. Another way of serving up fat is to pour it into yoghurt pots or half-coconut shells while warm. It can be mixed with bird food and kitchen scraps to make a nutritious "cake" (see page 29). This can then be suspended from a branch or bird-table.

Home projects

Home-made bird-tables need not be complex (see opposite). A simple tray on a post or suspended from the branches of a tree is all that is required to hold the food and keep it off the ground. Adding a roof helps to keep the

Drill holes *along the length of a log and smear and push fat into them. The log can then be hung from a tree or bush and attracts tits as well as other small species.*

To a visiting bird *like this Brambling, it is not the look of a table that matters, but the food and the location.*

Hanging half a coconut *makes a simple feeder; allow it to face downwards so that water does not collect.*

food dry and the table cleaner, but is not essential. If even this level of construction is daunting, however, try simply attaching a small tray to a windowsill. Although it may take birds some time to discover, many species will eventually become bold and approach the window, giving you unsurpassed views from within.

Seed hoppers keep food dry and stop it from blowing away in the wind. A simple hopper can be made using household materials (see opposite). Small versions can be fixed to trees or posts, while larger hoppers can be placed on the lawn for ground-feeding birds. The hopper can be filled with mixed seeds or small fruits, but remember to cover the jar with a piece of card while fitting it in place so that the contents do not spill out.

MAKING A BIRD-TABLE

First construct the tray: fix the side pieces to the base with 30mm (1¼in) rustproof nails. The side pieces do not butt together – leave gaps at each corner to allow rain to drain away. To make the roof, fit a piece of triangular dowel between the long edges of each roof panel so that they butt together neatly. Fix together with wood adhesive.

Cut the uprights from 20 x 20mm (¾ x ¾in) wood, and angle the top of each one by cutting off a 6mm (¼in) wedge. Nail the uprights into the corners of the tray. Attach triangular gables to the uprights, and then, finally, nail the roof to the structure.

Fix hooks to the roof and attach chains to hang the table from a tree

Completed bird-table

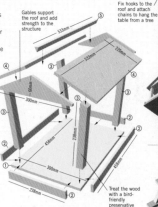

Gables support the roof and add strength to the structure

Treat the wood with a bird-friendly preservative

The table *can be mounted on a pole. This can be driven into the ground or a free-standing base can be constructed.*

The base *should be wide enough to form a stable support so that the table does not fall over in windy weather.*

Materials

① 12mm (½in) plywood
② 20mm (¾in) wood
③ 20 x 20mm (¾ x ¾in) wood
④ 9mm (⅜in) plywood
⑤ 9mm (⅜in) triangular dowel

MAKING A SEED HOPPER

This homemade hopper uses a 450g (1lb) jam jar, but the sizes of the back panel, base, and sides can be adjusted to fit other jars. Fix the back panel at a right angle to the base with long, rustproof screws. Attach the sides with nails to form a tray, leaving gaps at each corner for water drainage. Drill two holes in the base to fit the dowels, which steady the jar, and tack the webbing to the back panel to secure the jar. Screw three short screws into the base; the inverted jar rests upon them.

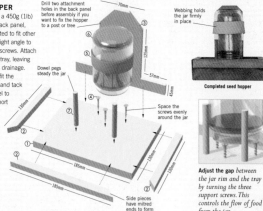

Drill two attachment holes in the back panel before assembly if you want to fix the hopper to a post or tree

Webbing holds the jar firmly in place

Completed seed hopper

Dowel pegs steady the jar

Space the screws evenly around the jar

Side pieces have mitred ends to form a neat corner

Adjust the gap *between the jar rim and the tray by turning the three support screws. This controls the flow of food from the jar.*

Materials

① 25mm (1in) wood
② 20mm (¾in) wood
③ 12mm (½in) plywood
④ Rustproof screws
⑤ Strip of webbing
⑥ Glass jar
⑦ 80mm (3in) dowel pegs

Bird-tables

THE TRADITIONAL BIRD-TABLE remains the most efficient feeder for the greatest number of common species, attracting birds as varied as Blackcaps, Coal Tits, and Collared Doves. Bird-tables do a simple job – keeping food off the ground and providing a safe place for birds to feed, but there are many variations on the basic design.

A well-stocked bird-table will reward its keeper with visits of less common species, such as this Bullfinch.

Table features

A well designed bird-table has a number of features that maximize the safety and comfort of visiting birds while preventing the loss and spoilage of food. It should be easy to clean and have good drainage (usually a base of stainless steel mesh) to prevent waterlogging. It should have raised edges to prevent food blowing away in strong winds, and be open in aspect, so that feeding birds can spot approaching predators and make their escape in good time.

A raised table will bring together small birds, such as Blue Tits and Great Tits, larger Starlings, and really big species like the Woodpigeon. Aggregations of birds that do not normally feed together may result in behaviour called "dominance", where some birds drive off others – even those larger than themselves. Blackcaps visiting bird-tables in the winter, for example, are notorious for driving other birds away from the feeding site.

BIRD-TABLE DESIGNS

Low bird-tables *attract birds like Pied Wagtails and Song Thrushes, which prefer to feed on the ground.*

A traditional *table attracts the most birds and the greatest diversity of species, including Blue Tits and Nuthatches.*

Metal bird-tables *may be more costly than wooden models, but they resist the elements more effectively.*

A tray hanging *from the branch of a tree can be very effective in attracting more timid species, such as Goldfinches.*

Mixed species *often feed together – a good opportunity to observe how different birds interact.*

STYLES TO AVOID

Certain designs of bird-tables are not suitable for wild birds and should be avoided. Tables with integral nest-boxes (right), for example, may seem a good idea, fulfilling two tasks in one, but in practice birds are very unlikely to nest where so many others feed in their territory. Tables that are enclosed or walled should be avoided too, because birds feel far less secure if they do not have clear sight of their surroundings. Tables should be easy to clean, without cracks and crevices in which food and excrement can collect.

Ideal locations

The classic bird-table is mounted on a pole set into the ground, but tables that hang from trees or wall brackets are just as effective. All types should be set up on lawns away from trees or shrubs that provide cover for cats, and far enough from overhanging branches to deter squirrels. At first, the table should be placed away from the house to minimize disturbance, but once the birds get used to feeding, it may be moved closer for better observation.

This popular type *of table has a heavy base for stability, yet can be moved easily round the garden if required.*

A roof protects *feeding birds from the worst of the winter weather, and an inverted metal collar below the table deters squirrels.*

A multi-tiered table *can hold several different types of food, so increasing the number and variety of visiting birds.*

This wall-mounted table *is made from sustainably-produced timber that has been treated with bird-safe preservative.*

Choosing bird food

OUR MOST FAMILIAR BIRDS naturally eat a wide variety of food. Song Thrushes feast on snails in summer, while Robins search for insects. Siskins take seeds from alder cones, and Blue Tits from silver birch catkins. By carefully choosing the food that we put out for birds, we can attract a range of visitors and help them survive through the year. Today, it is possible to choose from a vast range of proprietary bird foods or to make your own from seeds or kitchen scraps.

A hanging peanut feeder is a magnet to tits. The sturdy wire mesh prevents the nuts from being taken whole.

Energy to live

The amount that a bird needs to eat depends on the energy content of its food. Insects and other invertebrates are the most nutritious foods for birds, followed by seeds, and finally berries. A Blackbird feeding on cotoneaster in autumn, for example, must consume more than 300 individual berries in a day just to stay alive.

Proprietary bird foods usually consist of seeds or nuts. Mixtures are popular because they offer balanced nutrition similar to the birds' natural diet. The range of foods is enormous: free-flowing seed mixtures have been formulated for use in tubular feeders, there are special mixes for ground

Young birds benefit from the high-quality protein in live foods, such as mealworms.

feeders, and even "no mess" mixes from which seed husks have been removed. "Table seed" appeals to birds that prefer to eat off the bird table, such as Robins. There are mixes that contain oystershell grit – a good source of calcium which birds need to make egg shells – and mixtures specially developed for different types of birds, such as ducks, and swans.

Peanuts – perhaps the best-known bird food – should be used in purpose-built feeders that prevent birds such as tits and Nuthatches from taking entire nuts, which can choke nestlings. It is wise to buy peanuts from a reputable bird food supplier; they may otherwise contain aflatoxin – a poison produced by a fungus, which can kill birds.

PROPRIETARY BIRD FOOD

Safe, high-calorie, nutritious bird foods can be bought from specialist dealers. Seed mixes are the most popular, and attract the widest range of species, but pure single foods favour selected garden species. Dealers produce variety "starter packs", which allow you to experiment with different bird foods.

Nyjer seed is very attractive to Goldfinches, but due to its small size, it must be put in a special feeder or mixed with other foods.

Millet seed has a high fat content. Placed in ground feeders or on bird-tables, it appeals to smaller species, such as finches.

Black sunflower seeds are popular with many species including Greenfinches. Their husks can be added to the compost bin.

Feeder seed mix is a free-flowing mixture of sunflower seeds, chopped peanuts, millet, and oatmeal, suitable for hanging feeders.

Table seed mix for use on bird-tables contains wheat, sunflower seeds, kibbled maize, oatmeal, and chopped peanuts.

Peanuts are rich in oil and protein. They mainly attract tits, but are also popular with species such as Greenfinches and sparrows.

Raisins and sultanas are best when placed on a bird-table and mixed with other foods. A favourite of Blackbirds and thrushes.

Mealworms, waxworms, and earthworms placed in smooth, steep-sided bowls add a new dimension to bird feeding.

ANNUAL FEEDING REQUIREMENTS

Birds benefit from additional feeding year round, not just in the winter months. The amount of energy that a bird needs varies considerably through the year (see below); extra food is taken in when the calorific value of the food is low, when additional fat reserves are needed (for example before migration), and when feeding the young.

High food intake

Low food intake

SPECIES		Jan	Feb	Mar	Apr	May	Jun	Jul	Aug	Sep	Oct	Nov	Dec	PREFERRED FOOD
Collared Dove														*Mixed corn, seed mixes, table seed, grain.*
Dunnock														*Nyjer seed, pinhead oats.*
Robin														*Mealworms, waxworms, peanut granules, sunflower hearts.*
Song Thrush														*Fruit, earthworms, mealworms, peanut granules.*
Blackbird														*Fruit, peanut granules, mealworms, earthworms.*
Great Tit														*Peanuts, peanut cake, seed mixes, sunflower hearts.*
Blue Tit														*Peanuts, peanut cake, black sunflower seeds, seed mixes.*
Starling														*Scraps, seed mixes, peanut cake, live foods.*
House Sparrow														*Mealworms (when breeding), sunflower hearts, seed mixes.*
Chaffinch														*Peanut granules, sunflower hearts, seed mixes.*
Goldfinch														*Sunflower hearts, nyjer seed, black sunflower seeds, peanuts.*
Greenfinch														*Black sunflower seeds, sunflower hearts, seed mixes.*
Siskin														*Sunflower hearts, peanuts, black sunflower seeds, nyjer seed.*

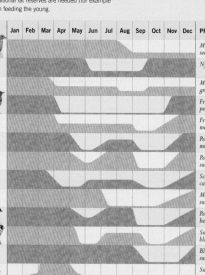

Making bird food

FEEDING GARDEN BIRDS need not be costly. Kitchen scraps are often rich in the very fats and carbohydrates that birds need to maintain vital reserves of body fat in the winter months. And even if proprietary seed mixes are used, they can be safely augmented with recycled food from our kitchens, or with windfall fruit. More dedicated bird gardeners may be inclined to make special bird cakes.

Food for free

Kitchen scraps placed on a bird-table will be eaten by a variety of species, from Robins to Song Thrushes. Bread, cake, and biscuit crumbs are all popular, as are cooked potato, cheese, and chopped bacon rind. Bones from cooked meats suspended from a bird-table will be pecked clean by Starlings and smaller species.

In autumn, windfall fruits can simply be left on the ground for the birds, or collected for use as a bird food later in the year. Fruit is popular with members of the thrush family, especially Blackbirds; any left over in late autumn may become food for migrant thrushes, such as Redwings and Fieldfares.

Smearing warm fat on a tree trunk, or pushing suet into a crack in a log makes a treat for Nuthatches and tits, while melted fat poured into a container and then pressed out on to the bird-table (or suspended on a string) provides energy-rich food for House Sparrows, Starlings, and tits. More complex home-made bird cakes (see opposite) will attract tits and finches.

Seeds from plants like flax, sunflower, beech, and teazel can be collected for use as bird food.

Once you start to provide food for birds, continue throughout the cold season, because the birds will begin to count on your offerings. It helps to keep the same food type at a particular feeder.

KITCHEN SCRAPS

Food for birds should be free from moulds, some of which can cause respiratory disease. Always remove any food that goes stale on the bird-table – it may contain salmonella, which can be fatal to birds like Greenfinches and House Sparrows.

Cake and bread should be soaked in water. They are good "filler" foods but lack the protein and fat that birds need in their diet, so should be used sparingly.

Cooked potatoes are high in protein. These left-overs are popular with many species, especially Starlings, which will peck out the soft centre, leaving the outer skin.

Cooked rice quickly vanishes from the bird-table, and is favoured by House Sparrows and Starlings. Avoid putting out rice that has been highly flavoured.

Fruits, such as apples, pears, and grapes are all popular foods. Thrushes, especially Blackbirds, Starlings, and tits all like to feed on fallen apples in late autumn.

Dry cheese is a protein-rich food that can be a life-saver for small birds in hard weather. Sprinkled under bushes it will sometimes be eaten by Wrens.

Bacon rind is popular with nearly all birds, and can attract larger species, such as Magpies and gulls. It should be cut into small pieces before serving.

Foods to avoid

Many food scraps are safe for birds, but some should be avoided. Uncooked rice and desiccated coconut, for example, will swell up inside a bird's gut, often with fatal results; for similar reasons, it is better to soak dry bread in water. Bacon rind is nutritious, especially uncooked, but may choke birds; it should be cut into small cubes, or secured firmly for birds to feed upon. Birds should not be given spoiled or spicy food, and most bird species do not cope with large amounts of salt, so salty fats, cured foods, crisps, and salted peanuts should be avoided.

While birds adore saturated fats, such as raw suet and lard, unsaturated fats may be harmful. These fats, which include margarine and vegetable oils, can become smeared on to the bird's body, where they destroy the waterproofing and insulating qualities of its feathers.

TABLE MANNERS

In nature, it is rare for birds to congregate frequently to feed at one spot. Busy bird-tables can become breeding grounds for diseases, some of which can be passed on to humans. Old food and droppings should regularly be scraped off, and the table washed with a mild detergent to prevent problems. Food scraps on the ground should also be cleared regularly to deter rodents.

Table scraper

Psittacosis *is a bacterial disease that can be transmitted from birds to humans, in whom it causes pneumonia-like symptoms.*

Making your own *bird cake is easy. Melt suet or dripping in a saucepan and add kitchen scraps, bird seeds, or unsalted peanuts, and pour into a container to set. The resulting cake can be put on to the bird-table.*

Drinking and bathing

WATER IS AN ESSENTIAL ingredient in any bird garden. It will attract a wide range of species throughout the year, including birds that feed elsewhere but need fresh water for drinking and bathing. The simplest way to provide water is in a bird-bath, but garden ponds with shallow edges provide the same facilities, with the added benefit of giving a home to aquatic animals.

A Goldcrest soaks itself while bathing, keeping its feathers in good order and keeping it cool in the heat.

The importance of water

Small birds, particularly those that feed on dry seeds, need to drink regularly (at least twice a day) to replace the fluids lost through respiration and in their droppings. Water is also essential for bathing and feather maintenance; dampening the feathers loosens the dirt and makes the feathers easier to preen.

The easiest way to provide water in the garden is in a bird-bath or a pond. A good bird-bath is simple and sturdy, but light enough to clean and refill. It must have sloping sides and a depth range between 2.5 and 10cm (1–4in) to allow every species to bathe at its ideal depth. The surface should be rough so birds can grip it with their claws, and it should be large enough to hold sufficient water to withstand a vigorous bathing session by a flock of Starlings. The simplest bird-bath is a large

WINTER WATER

In cold conditions, check your bird-bath daily. Break through the ice so that birds can bathe and drink. Avoid additives that prevent freezing, because these can poison birds or damage the waterproofing of their plumage. If possible, add a water feature such as a fountain; running water lets birds drink even when standing water is frozen. House Sparrows are particularly quick to take advantage of running water supplies.

A garden pond not only provides a place for birds to bathe and water for them to drink, but certain birds, like the Grey Heron, may even hunt for fish or frogs.

TYPES OF BIRD-BATH

A stone bath *on a pedestal has a traditional appearance, but is heavy, so difficult to move around the garden.*

Ceramic baths *may benefit from a thin layer of gravel on the bottom to give the birds a surer footing.*

This stone-effect *fibre-glass bath is light and easy to move. It has deep and shallow areas, so is suitable for birds of all sizes.*

Shallow metal containers *are fine, but water freezes quickly in cold weather. A floating tennis ball delays ice build-up.*

plant saucer with a stone in the middle to serve as a perch, or an inverted dustbin lid sunk into the ground; custom-made bird-baths are available from garden centres or specialist bird care suppliers. All types should be cleaned weekly to remove algae and droppings. Use dilute non-toxic disinfectant and rinse thoroughly.

Safety first

Birds are distracted while bathing, making them vulnerable to predator attack. Siting the bath near bushes or trees, where birds can retreat, perch, and preen, will attract more visitors, and planting thorny shrubs will keep cats away from the birds' cover.

During periods of drought, birds may try to use water barrels or troughs for drinking, and sadly many drown. If these containers cannot be covered, make them safer by floating a plank of wood on the water surface, so that birds can land and drink.

This shallow pond *edge attracts many Blackbirds in spring. The birds visit to drink, bathe, forage for food, and gather mud, which they use to build their nests.*

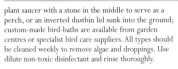

When bathing, *most garden birds crouch in the water, ruffle their feathers, and flick their wings, spreading the water over the body. After bathing they shake off the water and preen the feathers into position.*

Nest-boxes

EVEN IF A GARDEN IS WELL STOCKED with food, birds will leave in the breeding season unless they can find suitable nest sites. The way to keep birds in the garden year round is to put up nest-boxes that replicate the birds' natural nesting preferences. More than 60 species are known to use nest-boxes – from tits and Tree Sparrows, to Kestrels and Tawny Owls.

Enclosed and open boxes

Many garden birds prefer to nest in crevices in trees. Great Spotted Woodpeckers usually excavate their own holes, but other species either use old woodpecker nests or exploit natural cavities in old trees. In towns, where old trees are in short supply, the bird gardener can help by providing "enclosed" nest-boxes.

A typical box is rectangular, upright, with a small hole at the front. Its dimensions depend on the nesting species: small boxes attract tits, while the largest may be used by birds up to the size of Jackdaws. Social species may be tempted to a collection of several adjacent boxes, but most birds defend larger territories and prefer boxes spaced out around the garden.

"Open-fronted" nest-boxes are used by species that naturally nest on ledges and partly enclosed spaces – birds like Robins, Spotted Flycatchers, and Pied

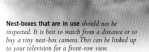

Nest-boxes that are in use *should not be inspected. It is best to watch from a distance or to buy a tiny nest-box camera. This can be linked up to your television for a front-row view.*

OPEN AND ENCLOSED NEST-BOXES

A half-open nest-box *is simple in design and easy to clean. They are particularly attractive to Robins, Spotted Flycatchers, and Wrens if positioned low down within dense cover.*

An open nest-box *gives species such as Blackbirds a platform on which they can build their nest. It is easy to maintain and offers excellent viewing opportunities.*

Tits prefer enclosed boxes *like this traditional style nest-box. Choose boxes with a hinged or removable roof or front panel to allow access for cleaning.*

CHOOSING A NEST-BOX

Nest-boxes are designed with various hole sizes suited to particular species. This table lists birds that prefer open and enclosed boxes, and the hole dimensions they require.

ENCLOSED NEST-BOXES		OPEN NEST-BOXES
Bird species	Diameter of hole	Bird species
Blue Tit	25mm (1in)	Wren
Great Tit	28mm (1in)	Pied Wagtail
Tree Sparrow	28mm (1in)	Robin
Nuthatch	32mm (1¼in)	Blackbird
House Sparrow	32mm (1¼in)	Spotted Flycatcher
Starling	45mm (1¾in)	Feral Pigeon
Great Spotted Woodpecker	50mm (2in)	Kestrel
Little Owl	70mm (2¾in)	
Mallard	150mm (6in)	
Stock Dove	150mm (6in)	
Tawny Owl	150mm (6in)	
Jackdaw	150mm (6in)	

Wagtails – and occasional Blackbirds and Wrens will also use this type of box.

When choosing a wooden nest-box, check that the exterior has been treated with preservative. Woodcrete boxes – made from a mixture of sawdust and concrete – are rot-proof; they are also better at maintaining internal temperature, and exclude most predators.

A House Sparrow *feeds its young. These birds rarely nest far away from buildings.*

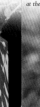

This tough resin nest-box *provides added safety for the nesting birds, because predators cannot enlarge the entrance hole to gain access to the eggs and chicks inside.*

This birch log nest-box *blends in perfectly with its rustic garden surroundings. The lid can be unscrewed for routine maintenance at the end of each nesting season.*

This three-hole woodcrete *box allows in additional light, encouraging birds to nest in the back of the box, out of the reach of predators. It is ideal for tits and Tree Sparrows.*

NEST-BOXES AND SPECIES RECOVERY

Some of our most familiar garden birds are in decline. House Sparrow populations, for example, have halved in some parts of Europe over the last 20 years. The use of suitable nest-boxes can locally boost numbers of these once-common birds. House Sparrows use Blue Tit-sized boxes, with entrance holes of 32mm (1¼in) diameter. Siting several nest-boxes close together in a garden may produce a visible increase in the sparrow population within a single year.

The Great Spotted Woodpecker *uses its tail as a prop when balancing on a tree trunk to excavate its hole or feed its young.*

Boxes should be put up in early January through to the end of February, when pairs of birds are already exploring potential nest sites. If a box is occupied, take care to minimize disturbance until the young take flight. After nesting, the nest material should be removed and the box disinfected to prevent a build-up of parasites (see opposite). The box should immediately be put back up again because it may be used in winter as a roost.

Do not despair if your nest-box is not used in the first year – chances are that it will be occupied in years

SPECIALIST NEST-BOXES

Kestrels naturally nest *on ledges on cliffs or buildings, or in large tree holes. They will sometimes occupy large, open nest-boxes sited high on mature trees.*

Starlings may appear *to be common, but European populations are in decline. Large nest-boxes with 45mm (1¾in) holes provide suitable nest sites.*

Tawny Owls *can be tempted to nest in long wooden boxes situated high in trees. Boxes must be well away from public places, because nesting owls sometimes swoop on passers by.*

to come. Putting up several boxes increases the chance of at least one being used, and by introducing a variety of styles there is a good chance that unusual species will arrive and nest; nest boxes also help species that are declining in their natural habitats (see opposite).

Rarer nesters
Some birds will almost never nest in artificial nest-boxes, and others have strict nesting requirements. Swifts, for example, nest almost entirely in niches in

Wrens are opportunists *when it comes to nesting. This one has found a good site in an old woolly jumper.*

HYGIENE AND NEST SITES
Most birds' nests harbour fleas and other parasites, which remain to infest young birds that hatch the following year, so old nests should be removed in late autumn. Boiling water can be used to clean the nest-box and kill any remaining parasites. Insecticides and flea powders must not be used. Placing a handful of clean hay or wood shavings (not straw) in the box once it is thoroughly dry increases the chances that it will be used in winter by small mammals or birds.

Opening a nest-box *in the breeding season could cause birds to abandon their eggs or young.*

the roofs of buildings, often in towns. Modern houses are built with few crevices for Swifts, yet putting up nest-boxes for the birds does not attract nesters. Studies showed that the Swifts often did not recognize the boxes as potential nest sites, but if they were played recordings of Swift calls, apparently originating from the boxes, this increased the chances of them investigating and then adopting a box.

Many specialist nest-boxes are used on nature reserves, but they are readily available and can be put up in suitable gardens (see below).

Swallows naturally *build bowl-shaped nests of mud lined with white feathers. Artificial nests made from a mix of wood and concrete (woodcrete) can be put inside a shed.*

Treecreepers usually *nest in narrow gaps and clefts in mature trees. Purpose-designed Treecreeper boxes are wedge shaped, and have unique triangular entrance holes.*

Dovecotes originally *held doves, to provide fresh meat throughout the winter, but today they are a highly decorative addition to any bird garden.*

Making nest-boxes

MAKING A NEST-BOX DOES NOT require great carpentry skills and can be fun. Design your box to suit the birds visiting your garden in winter and they may stay on to nest. There is no guarantee that a nest-box will attract birds, but careful siting increases the likelihood of it being adopted. Be patient: some boxes are not adopted for several years.

Position boxes facing away from the prevailing wind and out of the midday sun.

DIY nest-boxes

There are two basic designs of nest-box that can be made relatively simply: enclosed boxes with a small hole for tits, or open nest-boxes, favoured by Robins. Building your own nest-box means you can tailor it to a particular species; the size of an enclosed box and the diameter of its entrance hole, for example, will determine which species use it (see page 33).

Boxes should be made from strong timber and can be treated with a harmless wood preservative on the outside. Be sure that the cavity in the box is large enough for a nest and several young; boxes that are too small can lead to overcrowding, poor circulation, and over-heating in warm weather, while too large a space will simply be filled with more nesting material. At the end of each season, old nests need to be removed and the nest-box cleaned (see page 35). To allow access, fit them with a tight-fitting, hinged lid.

HOW TO BUILD A NEST-BOX

To make a standard enclosed nest-box, cut surplus floorboards or plywood into the sizes shown here. Saw the side of the lid that butts on to the back panel at an angle, so that it fits tightly to the back of the box. Secure a metal plate on the inside of the front panel to reinforce the hole. With 38mm (1½in) nails, fix the sides of the box to the edges of the base, then attach the front and back panels. Use a strip of waterproof material or a metal hinge to attach the lid to the back panel, and secure it with a hook and eye on each side panel.

Materials

① 15mm (⅝in) thick floorboard or plywood
② Metal plate or tin lid to reinforce the entrance hole
③ Metal hinge or strip of waterproof material

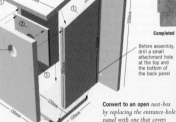

A piece of old bicycle inner tube makes an ideal waterproof "hinge"

Tailor the size of entrance hole to the bird species you want to attract

Completed enclosed nest-box

Before assembly, drill a small attachment hole at the top and the bottom of the back panel

Convert to an open *nest-box by replacing the entrance-hole panel with one that covers half of the front of the box.*

SITING NEST-BOXES

There are few hard and fast rules when it comes to choosing where to position nest-boxes around the garden. Birds like privacy when nesting, so nest-boxes should be put where there will be minimal disturbance and where predators, such as cats, find it difficult to attack. Installing several boxes increases the chance that one will be used, but as most species require a territory, they should be spaced out around the garden. It is a mistake to position nest-boxes too close to a bird-table or feeder, because it makes it more difficult for the resident birds to defend a territory around their home.

House Sparrows *prefer to nest close together, and use special "House Sparrow terraces" that allow several birds to nest in the same box.*

Starlings *use large enclosed nest-boxes with entrance holes 52mm (2in) in diameter. Position on a wall or tree.*

Treecreepers *naturally nest in gaps and crevices in trees, and use special wedge-shaped nest-boxes positioned on the trunk of a tree.*

Kestrels *nest in large open nest-boxes positioned near the top of a mature tree, or at least 5m (16ft) above the ground.*

House Martins *build their nests under the eaves of buildings and readily use specially designed boxes placed there, often returning year after year.*

Redstarts *are hole-nesters and may use enclosed nest-boxes. Try placing a box in a position that can be observed from inside your house.*

Nuthatches *use enclosed boxes with entrance holes 32mm (1¼in) in diameter. Position the box at least 2m (7ft) from the ground.*

Blue Tits *readily use enclosed nest-boxes. Angle the boxes downwards to prevent rain from entering.*

Great Tits *often use enclosed nest-boxes. Make sure there is an uninterrupted flight path to the entrance.*

Robins *use open nest-boxes placed in a sheltered position. Try hiding a box in the foliage of a climbing plant, such as ivy.*

Garden threats

ATTRACTING BIRDS INTO THE GARDEN is not always consistent with other activities around the home. For example, garden birds may be disturbed or attacked by domestic pets, endangered by chemicals used in the home or the garden, or injured in strikes with windows; birds are also threatened by other wild species. A few simple measures can help you avoid many of these problems, and maximize the benefits that your garden offers to wildlife.

Undesirable visitors

Many wild animals are tempted into gardens to take advantage of birds or bird foods: grey squirrels take bird seed, nuts, and also nestlings; rats and Magpies raid nests for eggs; and Sparrowhawks prey upon songbirds. In most cases, cages or baffles around feeders and bird-tables are enough to humanely deter the raiders.

The most dangerous garden visitors, however, are not wild animals, but domestic cats. Birds account for just 20 per cent of the animals they catch, but with an estimated 8 million cats in the UK alone, conservationists believe that they have a significant effect on wild bird populations.

Nest-boxes and feeders should always be positioned out of a cat's reach (see box, right). Cat repellents – either strong-smelling chemicals or ultrasonic devices – can be used to repel the hunters, although success is not guaranteed.

NEST PROTECTION

Predators are quick to make a meal out of a clutch of eggs or a brood of young. Siting nest-boxes high in trees, or surrounded by thorny shrubs (below) or tangles of chicken wire will make their approach more difficult. Nest-boxes can be fitted with plastic or metal "protectors" which lengthen the entrance hole, so preventing access by squirrels and cats. Metal plates around the entrance will prevent predators enlarging the holes to steal eggs.

Large glazed doors *are a danger; birds see the reflected sky and trees, and attempt to fly through. Stickers help to warn them off.*

Garden pesticides *rarely harm birds directly, but they kill the insects on which many birds depend. "Biological" pest control is better for birds.*

Mesh bags *should be avoided because they can trap birds' feet and break their legs. They also attract squirrels, which can open them easily.*

Grey squirrels *will exploit the easiest supply of food, even if this is eggs in a nest-box. Providing squirrels with their own cache of nuts may persuade them to leave birds and bird foods alone.*

Cat owners can *take measures to prevent their pets from catching birds. Cats should be kept indoors, around sunset and sunrise, when birds are most vulnerable. A simple bell, or a more sophisticated sonic device, attached to the collar, warns birds of the cat's approach.*

The bird-friendly garden

Changes in the countryside and in agricultural practices have made gardens a vitally important bird habitat. Maximizing your garden's appeal to birds is about making the most of what you already have, and planting with wildlife in mind.

Woodland gardens

ONE OF THE RICHEST NATURAL HABITATS for wildlife is the woodland edge, which offers a mix of vegetation, light and shade, and shelter. Birds have evolved to live in different sections of this habitat: Blue Tits in the tree canopy, Robins among the lower branches and bushes, and Dunnocks on the ground. There is space to create a woodland area even in a small courtyard garden.

The garden compromise

Creating a garden for birds is almost always a compromise. It may not even be worth trying to encourage birds if your garden is already a playground for small children or cats. Similarly, if you have serious horticultural objectives, it may be hard to reconcile your standards of neatness and planting with the more overgrown, unkempt look of a wildlife garden. But for most gardeners, a compromise is possible. Plants can be chosen that are attractive to both birds and humans, and cutting, pruning, and trimming can be reduced to allow insects to flourish and seeds and fruits to ripen.

Many garden birds *naturally prefer the mix of dense, tall foliage, tall herbs, and open space of the woodland edge (below). Shrubs and herbaceous beds in a garden (below right) can create the same effect.*

Maintaining a bird garden has become more acceptable in recent years as a natural outdoors look has become more fashionable. For example, the dead stems of perennials are now often left on the plants, because seedheads (with their rich load of bird food) and stems are considered to be decorative.

Hazels provide *good cover for nesting birds. Insects thrive in their foliage and the nuts are taken by some bird species.*

Natural engineering

To make a garden attractive for birds, try to recreate their natural habitat. For most of our common garden birds that means woodland — specifically, the boundary between woods and open ground, or the similar hedgerow habitat. To provide "natural" food

INSECT ATTRACTIONS

Hebes are decorative, evergreen shrubs that grow in sunny, well-drained places. They are planted in borders and rock gardens for their foliage and flowers. They are also a good food source for birds because they are attractive to insects, such as hoverflies and small bees. Insects of this size are the preferred prey for Spotted Flycatchers.

Spotted Flycatcher

Lavender *is grown for its fragrance and colour, but it also attracts Goldfinches, which eat its seeds.*

Dunnocks, but many more species will be attracted to carefully selected nest-boxes (see pages 32–35).

Creating a "woodland-edge" garden calls for long-term planning, because the plants brought into the garden need time to establish and grow; success is partly a case of trial and error, and partly dependent on your surrounding environment. Mistle Thrushes, for example, have recently expanded into suburban gardens. The reason for this has little to do with gardening practices, however, and more to do with the fact that amenity tree-planting is providing them with the high perches they need when singing.

Little Owls *are exciting visitors to gardens. Logpiles and compost heaps provide them with insects and worms.*

successfully, think about the year-round requirements of different birds. Choose annuals and herbaceous perennials, and some fast-growing lavender, cotoneaster, pyracantha, and bird cherry, which will quickly provide food and shelter. Plant fast-growing trees, such as birch, and replace walls with hedges, which will add wildlife value (see box below).

Dense bushes and climbers and taller trees will attract birds to nest, especially Blackbirds, Robins, and

HEDGE HABITATS

A well-established, *thick hedge provides ideal nesting and roosting sites, and is often the only hiding place in the garden. Hedges also provide better shelter from winds than solid walls and fences, preventing eddies that disturb nesting birds and that kill delicate plants.*

Any shrub *that stands being clipped can be trained to form a hedge. A mixture of fast-growing evergreens and broadleaf species is ideal.*

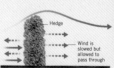

Incoming wind

Eddies make the garden blustery and draughty

Wall or fence

Hedge

Wind is slowed but allowed to pass through

Water gardens

WATER FEATURES CAN BE integrated into virtually any garden, whatever its size. Pools are used for drinking and bathing, and larger ponds may attract water birds. Muddy pond margins draw in species like wagtails, which come to forage for worms and insects, while Blackbirds, thrushes, and House Martins use pond mud for nesting material.

Moorhens may nest on garden ponds secluded by high vegetation. The pond should be at least 20m (66ft) square.

Attracted to water

Wildlife is drawn to ponds. The boundary between land and water, usually sheltered by dense foliage, presents an ideal habitat for a wide range of invertebrates, amphibians, and birds. Gardeners, too, adore water, because it allows the planting of exquisite water plants and exciting and attractive species that will only thrive in wet margins.

Pond construction

There are many ways to build a pond. The simplest is to lower a moulded fibreglass container into the ground, although these preformed ponds are limited in shape and size. Another alternative is to line a hole with impermeable clay, although this is most suited to the largest of ponds. Perhaps the best way to create a wildlife pond is to use thick neoprene sheeting to line a hole; today's long-lasting, inconspicuous pond liners make this a fairly straightforward process. Using flexible liner allows gradations of shape and depth.

A pond should have gently sloping sides; birds will drink and bathe in the shallows and the low gradient

Moving water features, such as waterfalls and fountains, prevent water from freezing in winter.

PLANNING AND PLANTING

When making a bird pond, leave shallow edges on at least part of the circumference, and plant them with marsh species, including flag irises, sedges, and marsh marigolds. The edges of the pond should shelve away gently so that a bird can wade in up to its middle. If this is not possible (for example, if using a pre-formed pond), build a platform from bricks or stones that is submerged just deep enough for birds to stand in.

Birds bathe in ponds year-round (above), but especially in winter when good feather maintenance is essential to keep warm. In the nesting season, some species collect mud as cement for their nests (left).

permits animals such as hedgehogs to clamber out. As a rule, the more varied the slopes and the longer the shoreline, the better the pond will be for wildlife. However, it should also have areas in which the depth exceeds 60cm (23in) deep, so that the water does not freeze solid in hard winters.

Position and stocking

Avoid siting the pond under trees – it will fill with autumn leaves and growing roots could puncture the pond lining. Instead, plant a low bush near the pond to provide cover for bathing birds. Do not automatically place your pond in a wet or damp hollow where wildlflife may already be present; having more than one wet area in a garden can increase the variety of wildlife.

The pond is incomplete without plants. Plant in late spring when the water is beginning to warm up. Submerge the plants in plastic baskets or flowerpots and, if necessary, weight the pots with stones until the trapped air has dispersed. The weights may need to be retained for tall plants that will be blown over by the wind. Place the containers on bricks so that the leaves are at surface level. The plants can gradually be lowered as the leaves spread. Only one or two plants are needed for a small pond.

Pondweed adds interest to the surface of the water, while marginal plants such as sedges, purple loosestrife, and kingcups provide colour and variety around the edge of a pond. Tall waterside plants may help attract shyer birds and deter herons, which like a clear view of their surroundings.

A freshly-filled pond is barren at first, but life soon appears in the form of water beetles, dragonflies, and other insects that fly in and settle. Frogs, toads, and newts may also discover the pond for

Amphibians are good colonizers, and appear once your pond is established. Newts favour ponds next to wild areas with plants like water forget-me-not.

Bulrushes provide birds with food and nesting material. Their seedheads attract feeding birds in autumn.

themselves and establish populations. Snails, and other animals that are aquatic rather than amphibious, have to be introduced from another pond. Populations of creatures such as water fleas, which are food for larger animals, can be started by adding a bucket of water and mud from a well-established pond. Fish, such as sticklebacks, are an interesting addition, but check that the species you choose do not eat tadpoles.

A natural pond (below) takes years to develop into a focus for wildlife. If designed carefully, a garden pond (below right) can reproduce these conditions.

Easy gardens

PEOPLE WITH GARDENS are not necessarily keen gardeners. Some prefer to maintain their garden rather like their home, tidying regularly but refurbishing rarely. This approach is highly compatible with wildlife gardening because birds are most likely to be attracted to less "managed" areas with weed seeds and insects. However, this does not mean that a wildlife garden is a neglected garden.

Soil and aspect

The key to maintaining a successful wildlife garden with minimum effort is to adapt to local conditions. Use bird-friendly plants that are sympathetic with the soil type and aspect of your garden. For example, if your soil is poor and dry, don't try to enrich it with fertilizer; instead, give it a Mediterranean look with lavender and aromatic herbs. If your garden is shady, typical woodland floor plants will come into their own.

Practise sensible, low-intensity cultivation. Do not trim all your herbaceous plants in the autumn, because they provide shelter for insects

later in the season. Similarly, do not clear away all fallen leaf litter; it can be home to ground beetles and centipedes. Regularly mulch any areas of bare soil with bark chippings to control weeds and encourage earthworms.

If you have a large lawn, give parts of it no more than two or three cuts a year. This will allow broad-leaved plants to flower and set seed amongst the grass – excellent food for birds. In summer, your flower-rich lawn will swarm with insects that help feed hungry broods, but remember that the grass should be cut before it turns into hay and becomes untidy. Grass can also be allowed to grow and seed

Fat hen *is an annual weed, not loved by gardeners, but its seeds are an important food for many birds.*

Working with the garden *means considering light and soil conditions. Shade-tolerant plants work in a walled or woodland garden (below), while plants like gorse thrive on acid soils (right).*

around trees and in tight corners; the long growth gives shelter to animals, from insects and snails to mice and voles, which may, in turn, attract birds of prey.

Native or exotic?

Most successful wildlife gardens are well stocked with native plants. These species have evolved hand-in-hand with native animals, so provide the habitat that resident wildlife needs. For example, teazel and thistles provide birds with seeds, flowers such as

A damp, grassy patch can be transformed into a flower-rich meadow, attractive for birds, bees, and butterflies. It can be planted with flowers such as the fritillary (right).

foxgloves and lavender yield nectar to attract bees, and native trees, such as rowan and elder, produce berries. Grass species, such as fescues and bents, provide seeds for sparrows and continue to feed birds through the winter. Plants with "flat" flowers, such as sedums and *Limnanthes douglasii*, attract hoverflies and lacewings.

Native species are the obvious choice, but exotics can also be valuable in the wildlife garden. Verbena (*Verbena bonariensis*), for example, is a native of South America. Its seeds are eaten by finches and tits, and it produces plenty of nectar, which is a great draw for butterflies and hoverflies, and these, in turn, draw in hunting birds. Choosing exotic plants allows you to extend the growing season in your garden, making it attractive to birds through out the year. However, when choosing exotics, take care to avoid invasive species such as the common rhododendron.

CHOOSING PLANTS

Selecting plants for your garden calls for research. You must take into account soil type, aspect, and maintenance, as well as a plant's size, appearance, and value to wildlife. The following pages list a handful of species of known value to birds. In general, you should choose old-fashioned, single varieties, because modern, double petal varieties produce little or no nectar. Also, remember that varieties which are susceptible to attack by caterpillars and other insects may be the best choices for planting in bird gardens.

Primroses are *native plants that spread naturally in gardens. They bring colour in spring in a variety of soil and shade conditions.*

Buddleia is an exotic *plant that is easy to grow. It produces copious nectar and is a favourite of butterflies and other insects.*

Before buying, *check plants for vigorous, balanced growth and healthy leaves. Look at the roots, by easing the plant out of the pot if possible, to see if they are overcrowded.*

Soil held firmly around the roots

Well-established root system

Choose a bare-root *tree or shrub with roots spread evenly around the stem. It should have plenty of small "feeder" roots.*

Bare-rooted plants must be planted when dormant

Fibrous "feeder" roots

Plant guide: trees

Trees provide nesting places, song-posts, and an important variety of foods for birds in the garden. Growing a tree is a long-term investment, but choosing fast-growing or smaller species will give a quicker return. Larger species can be coppiced to make them more suitable for garden use. Choose species carefully: years can be wasted if the tree does not flourish in the conditions in your garden.

Silver birch
Betula pendula

Grown for its attractive silvery bark and golden leaves in autumn, this tree is suitable for smaller gardens because it will coppice. It casts light shade and is tolerant of poor and acid soils. It supports over 200 types of insect, and birds eat its winged seeds. The trunk is good for woodpecker nest holes.

HEIGHT 20m (66ft) **SPREAD** 10m (33ft)

CULTIVATION Grows in dry soil in a sunny position. Do not grow near buildings or other trees, because its roots grow near the surface.

RELATED SPECIES Monarch birch (*B. maximowicziana*) is a quick-growing species; *B.* var *jacquemontii* has very white bark.

Alder
Alnus glutinosa

This deciduous tree is suitable for medium or large gardens. Birds, such as Siskins, eat the seeds when the woody cone-shaped fruits open.

HEIGHT 25m (83ft) **SPREAD** 10m (33ft)

CULTIVATION Grows in moderately fertile, moist soil. It can be coppiced.

RELATED SPECIES Italian alder (*A. cordata*) grows on dry soil; grey alder (*A. incana*) thrives in cold, poor soils; *A. i.* 'Aurea' has yellow foliage and red catkins.

Bird cherry
Prunus padus

A small deciduous tree with fragrant white flowers. These develop into bitter, black cherries that are enjoyed by many birds, including Hawfinches.

HEIGHT 15m (50ft) **SPREAD** 10m (33ft)

CULTIVATION Prefers full sun and grows in moist but well-drained soil. Its shallow roots hinder underplanting, and it throws up suckers.

RELATED SPECIES Some *Prunus* varieties do not produce fruit. Wild cherry (*P. avium*), the ancestor of cultivated cherries, is a common garden tree.

Crab apple
Malus sylvestris

This small tree is suitable for smaller gardens. The fruit and seeds are eaten by birds, such as Blackbirds, and the leaves support caterpillars.

HEIGHT 10m (33ft) **SPREAD** 10m (33ft)

CULTIVATION Prefers full sun but will grow in part-shade, in any soil. Prune in winter.

RELATED SPECIES *M. sylvestris* is the ancestor of cultivated apple species (*M. domestica*). *M.* 'John Downie' and the Siberian crab apple (*M. baccata*) retain fruit on the tree into late winter.

Rowan
Sorbus aucuparia

The red-orange berries of this small, deciduous tree are eaten by many birds; if there is a good crop, Fieldfares and Waxwings may delay migration.

HEIGHT 15m (50ft) **SPREAD** 8m (26ft)

CULTIVATION Prefers sun or light-dappled shade and needs moist, light soil. It will tolerate extreme acidity.

RELATED SPECIES Wild service tree (*S. torminalis*) and whitebeam (*S. aria*; good in chalky soils) will grow in gardens; service tree (*S. domestica*).

Holly
Ilex aquifolium

A small evergreen that grows in hedges and woods. The flowers open in May and June; the red or yellow berries are eaten by many birds.

HEIGHT 3–15m (10–50ft)
SPREAD 5m (17ft)

CULTIVATION Grows in sun or shade, and withstands pollution and salt spray.

RELATED SPECIES *I. a.* 'Argentea Longifolia' is good for berries.

Goat willow
Salix caprea

This deciduous, fast-growing tree bears catkins in late winter, attracting early insects. Blue Tits will drink the nectar, and finches eat its seeds.

HEIGHT 10m (33ft) **SPREAD** 8m (26ft)

CULTIVATION Prefers full sun, and can grow in dry, but not chalk, soil. It coppices freely, and cuttings will readily take root. Site away from drains which can be invaded by roots.

RELATED SPECIES Grey willow (*S. cinerea*) is similar but smaller and more bushy.

European larch
Larix decidua

This deciduous larch bears cones which ripen in autumn, shedding seeds that attract many birds, including Great Spotted Woodpeckers.

HEIGHT 50m (165ft) **SPREAD** 5–15m (17–50ft)

CULTIVATION This fast-growing tree prefers full sun and deep, well-drained soils. Avoid wet soils and dry, shallow chalk.

RELATED SPECIES Fast-growing and disease-free Japanese larch (*L. kaempferi*) and hybrid larch (*L. x. eurolepis*) are commonly grown.

Common lime
Tilia x europaea

A tall deciduous tree that is a natural, fertile hybrid. Insect-eating birds are attracted to the aphids on its leaves, while other birds enjoy the seeds.

HEIGHT 35m (116ft) **SPREAD** 15m (50ft)

CULTIVATION Grows in sun or part-shade in moist but drained soils. It is suitable for lopping and coppicing.

RELATED SPECIES Silver lime (*T. tomentosa*) and pendant silver lime (*T.* 'Petiolaris') have leaves with silver undersides.

Common oak
Quercus robur

Suitable only for large gardens, this slow-growing, deciduous tree is an important resource for birds. It supports more insect species than any other European tree, including caterpillars, which are vital for nesting birds, and the acorns are eaten by a variety of birds.

HEIGHT 30–40m (99–132ft)
SPREAD 25m (83ft)

CULTIVATION Grows in deep soil in a well-drained position. It retains dead leaves through winter until it reaches 2.5m (8ft) in height.

RELATED SPECIES Fast-growing red oak *Q. r. rubra* survives air pollution.

Jay

Plant guide: shrubs

Shrubs are used by gardeners to give structure and colour to the garden, and for hedging. A shrub is essentially a small tree, but the term is used more for a woody plant that produces a mass of branches from the base rather than a single trunk. Certain trees can be pruned to grow as shrubs. Like trees, shrubs are valuable for birds, their dense growth providing shelter for nesting and roosting.

Cotoneaster
Cotoneaster microphyllus

An evergreen shrub with rigid, often drooping, branches. The small leaves make dense cover; it bears red fruits which are popular with many birds.

HEIGHT 1m (3½ft) **SPREAD** 2m (7ft)

CULTIVATION Prefers dry sites in sun or part-shade. Good for seaside sites.

RELATED SPECIES Prostrate *C. horizontalis* is good for walls, banks, and ground cover, especially in small gardens; *C. dammeri* is ideal for banks and ground cover beneath other shrubs.

Blackthorn (sloe)
Prunus spinosa

Common in hedgerows and woods, this small shrub or tree bears masses of small white flowers. The round, shiny black fruit – the sloe – remains on the tree through the winter and is enjoyed by a variety of birds. The dense foliage provides good nesting places.

HEIGHT 4m (13ft) **SPREAD** 3m (10ft)

CULTIVATION Prefers full sun, and soil that is neither waterlogged nor too acid. Trim in winter, once the nesting season is over.

RELATED SPECIES Bullace (*Prunus domestica*) is a hybrid that grows in the British Isles.

Hawthorn (may)
Crataegus monogyna

This small, deciduous tree is often used for hedging. The crimson berries, or haws, are eaten by many birds, the leaves by some Woodpigeons.

HEIGHT 10m (33ft)
SPREAD 8m (26ft)

CULTIVATION Prefers sun but will grow in shade, and will grow in polluted or exposed sites.

RELATED SPECIES *C. laevigata* is useful for garden hedging.

Firethorn
Pyracantha coccinea

A dense, spiny, evergreen shrub, which can be grown in a hedge or against a wall. The berries are eaten by some birds, but its value is as a site for nests.

HEIGHT 2m (7ft) **SPREAD** 2m (7ft)

CULTIVATION Prefers sun or part-shade and grows in any well-drained soil. Train against a wall with trellis or wires for support.

RELATED SPECIES *P.* 'Golden Dome' forms a dense mound with yellow berries; *P. angustifolia* grows on north-facing walls.

Juneberry (serviceberry)
Amelanchier lamarckii

The foliage of this deciduous shrub or tree turns from green or bronze to red and orange in autumn. The clusters of berries are popular with birds.

HEIGHT 6m (20ft) **SPREAD** 3m (10ft)

CULTIVATION Requires full sun or part-shade, and prefers moist or well-drained, fairly acid soil. Prune during winter to keep plant shape.

RELATED SPECIES *A. arborea*, *A. laevis*, and *A. canadensis* are similar species that are often confused with *A. lamarckii*.

Elder
Sambucus nigra

This deciduous shrub or small tree bears purple-black berries that are extremely popular with birds. It can become rampant if left unchecked.

HEIGHT 4m (13ft) **SPREAD** 4m (13ft)

CULTIVATION Needs a sunny position and moist, fertile soil. Prune old shoots in winter and dig out unwanted seedlings.

RELATED SPECIES *S. n.* 'Aurea' is smaller and less rampant than the native species; it has attractive gold foliage and is very hardy.

Yew
Taxus baccata

Often used for hedging, this evergreen tree has dense foliage of dark green, flattened leaves. It bears bright red, fleshy, cup-shaped fruits, or arils, each containing a single green seed. These are enjoyed by many birds; all parts of yew, however, are poisonous to humans.

HEIGHT 15m (50ft) **SPREAD** 10m (33ft)

CULTIVATION Grows almost anywhere in sun or shade and is tolerant of drought, exposure, and polluted air.

RELATED SPECIES *T. b.* 'Dovastonii Aurea' has golden foliage and grows to 5m (17ft); *T. cuspidata* is dwarf and very hardy.

Greenfinch

Mezereon
Daphne mezereum

This deciduous shrub bears fragrant pink flowers. In May and June, its round, yellow fruits are eaten by many birds; Blackcaps drink its nectar.

HEIGHT 1m (3½ft) **SPREAD** 1m (3½ft)

CULTIVATION Grows in moderately fertile, well-drained soil in full sun. Mulch regularly to keep the roots cool, but keep pruning to a minimum as it is prone to die-back.

RELATED SPECIES *D. m.* 'Alba' has white flowers and translucent amber fruits.

Hazel
Corylus avellana

A deciduous shrub that bears long, yellow male catkins in January. The nuts are eaten by several birds, including Nuthatches.

HEIGHT 6m (20ft)
SPREAD 6m (20ft)

CULTIVATION Prefers sun or part-shade and well-drained soil but grows wild on damp soils. Nuts are borne after seven years.

RELATED SPECIES Corkscrew hazel (*C. a.* 'Contorta') has strangely twisted twigs.

Privet
Ligustrum vulgare

Ideal for hedging, this fast-growing, deciduous shrub bears white, scented flowers that attract insects, and black berries eaten by many birds.

HEIGHT 5m (17ft) **SPREAD** 3m (10ft)

CULTIVATION Prefers well-drained, limestone soil and full sun. Hard cutting improves its value as cover for nests but leave untrimmed for fruit.

RELATED SPECIES Japanese privet (*L. japonicum*) and golden privet (*L. ovalifolium* 'Aureum') are suitable for ornamental hedges.

Guelder rose
Viburnum opulus

A deciduous shrub or small tree that produces clusters of white flowers in spring, followed by scarlet fruits, which are eaten by a variety of birds, including Waxwings and Bramblings.

HEIGHT 4m (13ft) **SPREAD** 4m (13ft)

CULTIVATION Prefers fertile, moist but well-drained soil in full sun or part-shade.

RELATED SPECIES The wayfaring tree (*V. lantana*) is suitable for gardens and is good on chalk; *V. o.* 'Compactum' is slow-growing and dense.

Waxwing

Blackcurrant
Ribes nigrum

A deciduous shrub cultivated for its soft fruit. The small black berries ripen in June and July and are popular with many birds, including Blackbirds.

HEIGHT 2m (7ft) **SPREAD** 2m (7ft)

CULTIVATION Grows in moderately fertile soil in full sun. It can be trained against a wall. After fruiting, cut out old stems.

RELATED SPECIES Redcurrant (*R. rubrum*) and gooseberry (*R. uva-crispa*) are close relatives also cultivated for their fruits.

Dogwood
Cornus sanguinea

With its bold red twigs, this deciduous bush or small tree gives winter colour to the garden. The small black berries are popular with several bird species.

HEIGHT 4m (13ft) **SPREAD** 3m (10ft)

CULTIVATION Grows in fertile, chalky soil, and needs a sunny position to produce red stems. It grows from suckers so will colonize an area without assistance.

RELATED SPECIES *C. canadensis* grows in acid soil and is suitable for ground cover.

Oregon grape
Mahonia aquifolium

This evergreen shrub bears yellow, fragrant flowers, which are visited for their nectar and pollen. The blue-black berries are eaten by Blackbirds.

HEIGHT 1m (3½ft) **SPREAD** 1.5m (5ft)

CULTIVATION Prefers some shade. Cut down old stems in April.

RELATED SPECIES Varieties range from the 3m (10ft) *M. japonica* to the 30cm (12in) *M. repens*, which spreads by underground stems.

Barberry
Berberis vulgaris

An evergreen shrub with sharp spines and finely branching twigs, suitable for hedging. It bears orange-red berries that are eaten by many birds.

HEIGHT 4m (13ft) **SPREAD** 4m (13ft)

CULTIVATION Grows in sun or part-shade and in almost any well-drained soil. Full sun produces the best autumn colours. Good for seaside sites.

RELATED SPECIES The evergreen *B. darwinii* is good for hedging and is attractive to birds; *B. coryi* is suitable for small gardens.

Beech
Fagus sylvatica

Often grown as a hedge, this deciduous tree provides places for birds to nest and roost. The seeds are important for several bird species.

HEIGHT 30m (99ft) **SPREAD** 25m (83ft)

CULTIVATION Grows in well-drained, chalky soil, and prefers a sunny position or part-shade. When grown as a hedge, trim in summer. Trees under 2.5m (8ft) in height keep their leaves in winter.

RELATED SPECIES Copper beech (*F. s.* var. *purpurea*) has purple-brown leaves.

Spindle
Euonymus europaeus

A small, deciduous shrub grown for its autumn leaf colour and bright seed pods. The seeds are eaten by many bird species, including finches.

HEIGHT 6m (20ft) **SPREAD** 2m (7ft)

CULTIVATION Grows in full sun or part-shade, and prefers calcareous soils.

RELATED SPECIES *E. fortunei* var. *radicans* is a creeper that provides good ground cover; Japanese spindle (*E. japonicus*) is evergreen and tolerates air pollution and salt spray.

Bay laurel
Laurus nobilis

This evergreen shrub, often grown in containers, has shiny, green leaves and bears small black berries. The dense foliage provides useful nesting places.

HEIGHT 12m (40ft) **SPREAD** 10m (33ft)

CULTIVATION Grows in full sun or part-shade in fertile, well-drained soil. It should be sheltered from strong winds and watered in dry weather.

RELATED SPECIES Cherry laurel (*Prunus laurocerasus*) and Portugal laurel (*P. lusitanica*) are cherries that look similar to bay laurel.

Lavender
Lavandula angustifolia

The flowers of this highly aromatic, evergreen shrub have a high nectar content and attract many insects; the seeds are eaten by finches; and the long stems make good nesting material.

HEIGHT 30–60cm (12–23in)
SPREAD 30–60cm (12–23in)

CULTIVATION Prefers a sunny position and fertile, well-drained soil. Trim in spring to maintain compactness and the overall shape of the shrub.

RELATED SPECIES French lavender (*L. stoechas*) is also grown in gardens.

Goldfinch

Garrya
Garrya elliptica

A dense, evergreen shrub grown for its dramatic, long grey catkins in late winter. It is valuable for birds because it provides good cover for early nests.

HEIGHT 4m (13ft) **SPREAD** 4m (13ft)

CULTIVATION Can be grown in part-shade against a wall even in poor soil, but it prefers a well-drained soil. It can tolerate salt spray, but requires protection from frosts and strong winds. It should be pruned only to maintain shape.

RELATED SPECIES None.

Plant guide: climbers

Climbers provide a simple way of adding to the vertical dimension of the garden, especially where there is too little space to grow trees. They are indispensable for covering unsightly buildings or even bare ground, and add flowers, fruit, and foliage to bare walls, pergolas, and pillars. While some yield fruit that attracts birds, their main value is in providing cover for roosting and nesting.

Ivy
Hedera helix

This evergreen climber clings to trees or walls and provides good cover for nesting and roosting. Its berries are a valuable winter food for many birds.

HEIGHT 10m (33ft)

CULTIVATION Tolerates shade but only flowers in the sun and prefers well-drained soils.

RELATED SPECIES *H. h.* 'Cavendishii' is good for growing against walls.

Golden hop
Humulus lupulus

This herbaceous, twining climber has male and female flowers on separate plants. The female flowers develop into clusters of hops, which are used in brewing. Golden hop provides valuable cover for nests and roosts.

HEIGHT 5m (17ft)

CULTIVATION Grows in sun or part-shade in humus-rich soil. Water well in dry weather. Support the stems and cut back in spring.

RELATED SPECIES None.

Honeysuckle
Lonicera periclymenum

Grown for its scented flowers, this twining climber attracts insects and Blackcaps, which drink the nectar. The berries are popular with many birds.

HEIGHT 7m (23ft)

CULTIVATION Grow in sun or shade on fertile soil. Immediately after flowering, thin and cut back old flowering shoots to 1cm (½in) of old wood.

RELATED SPECIES *L. pileata* is good in shade; *L. nitida* is a dense, quick-growing, evergreen shrub; *L. fragrantissima* is a winter-flowering shrub.

Virginia creeper
Parthenocissus quinquefolia

This quick-growing, deciduous climber clings to supports with tendrils. It provides cover for nests and the berries are eaten by some birds.

HEIGHT 20m (66ft)

CULTIVATION Will grow in shade or part-shade. Support young growth until it clings to supports. Trim in early spring to restrain and direct the growth of this vigorous climber.

RELATED SPECIES Chinese Virginia creeper (*P. henryana*) is good for ground cover.

Grape vine
Vitis vinifera

A cultivated fruit crop in many parts of the world, this climber bears clusters of green, red, or purple fleshy fruits, enjoyed by many birds.

HEIGHT 30m (99ft)

CULTIVATION Requires full sun and rich soil, and can be trained on trellises, pergolas, or against walls. Protect against late frost.

RELATED SPECIES The ornamental vine *V. v.* 'Purpurea' has inedible fruit.

Blackberry (bramble)
Rubus fruticosus

A perennial, deciduous climber whose prickles act as hooks to anchor the stems as they scramble over each other or up trees and shrubs. It bears white flowers in summer, and plump black fruits in early autumn.

HEIGHT 3m (10ft) **SPREAD** 3m (10ft)

CULTIVATION Grows in fertile, well-drained soil and prefers sun, but evergreen varieties tolerate shade. Blackberries grown for their fruit are trained against a wall or wires and stems are cut to the ground after flowering. To provide nesting places for birds, blackberry stems should be left to form a thicket, if space allows.

RELATED SPECIES Dewberry (*R. caesius*), cloudberry (*R. chamaemorus*), and raspberry (*R. idaeus*) bear edible fruits.

Blackcap

Dog rose
Rosa canina

A deciduous, scrambling shrub that bears red, fleshy fruits (hips), attracting finches, tits, and other birds. Bushy growth make good nest sites.

HEIGHT 3m (10ft)

CULTIVATION Prefers sun and fertile soil. Occasionally trim to shape or thin in winter. Prune in February to allow fruiting.

RELATED SPECIES *R. rugosa* bears large hips, which are popular with many bird species.

Climbing hydrangea
Hydrangea petiolaris ssp petiolaris

A deciduous, woody climber that clings to walls by aerial roots on the stems. The tangle of stems can give valuable shelter to birds.

HEIGHT 7m (23ft) **SPREAD** 7m (23ft)

CULTIVATION Grows in sun or part-shade, and will thrive against a north-facing wall. In dry soil, it requires a more shady position. It is self-clinging, and can be pruned after flowering.

RELATED SPECIES *H. aspera* and *H. macrophylla* are bushy species.

Wisteria
Wisteria chinensis

Grown for its dramatic, drooping purple flowers, this deciduous climber has thick, woody stems, which make good supports for birds' nests.

HEIGHT 30m (99ft)

CULTIVATION Grows best in full sun (with its roots shaded) in a well-drained soil. It can be trained to wire attached to a wall, and will cover a pergola. Prune after flowering.

RELATED SPECIES Japanese wisteria (*W. floribunda*) produces very long, purple blooms.

Clematis
Clematis montana

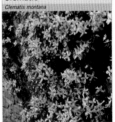

This evergreen climber produces a mass of small white flowers in spring. It provides good cover; its seeds and buds are eaten by some birds.

HEIGHT 12m (40ft) **SPREAD** 3m (10ft)

CULTIVATION A vigorous, hardy climber that will grow in sun or shade, but will flower best in a sunny postion. Plant in well-drained soil, and prune in May or June, after flowering.

RELATED SPECIES *C. alpina* is suitable for north-facing or very exposed sites.

Plant guide: herbaceous plants

Herbaceous plants are an important part of any garden designed to attract wildlife. In summer, the wide variety of invertebrates attracted to their flowers and foliage is appreciated by many insect-eating bird species, while the seeds they produce are an important food source for birds. Allow seedheads to ripen and stand until the seeds are shed, and they will provide food for birds into the winter months.

Angelica
Angelica sylvestris

This tall perennial herb grows in damp places. The white or pink flowers heads attract many insects, while the seeds are eaten by tits and finches.

HEIGHT 2m (7ft) **SPREAD** 1m (3½ft)

CULTIVATION Grows in sun or shade, in damp soil. Sow in autumn or spring and, after flowering, allow seeds to form. Best grown as a biennial, it will self-seed freely.

RELATED SPECIES Archangel (*A. archangelica*) is native to northern Europe.

Red clover
Trifolium pratense

Considered a weed when growing in a lawn, this low-growing perennial herb is a colourful addition to a stretch of garden meadow. The pink-purple flower heads appear between May and September. Several bird species feed on the seeds, and Woodpigeons also eat the leaves.

HEIGHT 20cm (8in) **SPREAD** 20cm (8in)

CULTIVATION Naturally invades the garden but can be grown from seed. It grows best in well-drained soil in full sun, and self-seeds very readily.

RELATED SPECIES *T. incarnatum* has red-yellow flowers.

Amaranth
Amaranthus caudatus

Commonly known as love-lies-bleeding, amaranth is an annual grown for its flowers and colourful foliage. Many birds eat its seeds.

HEIGHT 1.2m (4ft) **SPREAD** 45cm (18in)

CULTIVATION Sow seeds under glass in March or in a sunny, sheltered site in April.

RELATED SPECIES Joseph's coat (*A. tricolor*) is grown for its multi-coloured foliage.

Field forget-me-not
Myosotis arvensis

This small annual or biennial bears small, bright blue flowers from April to September. The tiny seeds are popular with finches.

HEIGHT 15cm (6in) **SPREAD** 10cm (4in)

CULTIVATION Prefers sun and well-drained soil. Cultivated forms are sown as seed in autumn, or bought as bedding plants.

RELATED SPECIES Water forget-me-not (*M. scorpoides*) is suitable for bog gardens; *M. sylvatica* is a cultivated species.

Argentinian vervain
Verbena bonariensis

A favourite for attracting butterflies and other insects, this perennial's seeds also attract Greenfinches, Goldfinches, and Blue Tits.

HEIGHT 1.5m (5ft) **SPREAD** 50cm (20in)

CULTIVATION Prefers sun and well-drained soil. Sow seeds in autumn and spring. Divide clumps in spring, when necessary.

RELATED SPECIES *V. alpina* is a low spreading perennial; *V. x hybrida* is slow-growing and is cultivated as an annual.

Teazel
Dipsacus fullonum

This short-lived perennial herb bears heads of tiny purple flowers. In winter, Goldfinches extract seeds from the dead seedheads.

HEIGHT 2m (7ft) **SPREAD** 60cm (23in)

CULTIVATION Grows in moderately fertile soil, including clay, in sun or part-shade.

RELATED SPECIES Fuller's teazel (*D.f.* subsp. *sativus*) is grown for its stiff, spiny seedheads which are used for raising the nap of cloth.

Common nettle
Urtica dioica

With its stinging leaves and rapid growth, the nettle is considered a nasty weed, but it attracts caterpillars and the birds that feed on them.

HEIGHT 1.5m (5ft) **SPREAD** 15cm (6in)

CULTIVATION Grows best in rich, well-manured soil, but should only be planted in a confined area. Cut mature stems to promote fresh growth for caterpillars.

RELATED SPECIES Annual nettle (*U. urens*) is a smaller, less invasive species.

Evening primrose
Oenothera biennis

A biennial herb grown for the succession of short-lived yellow flowers. The flowers attract insects and the seeds are eaten by finches.

HEIGHT 1m (3½ft) **SPREAD** 40cm (16in)

CULTIVATION Needs full sun and well-drained soil. Self-seeds and can be divided in spring.

RELATED SPECIES *O. acaulis* and Ozark sundrops (*O. macrocarpa*) are 15cm (6in) high and suit small gardens.

Greater plantain
Plantago major

In gardens, this perennial herb is a weed that grows on lawns and in gravel paths. If left uncut, its seeds may be eaten by buntings and finches.

HEIGHT 30cm (12in) **SPREAD** 60cm (23in)

CULTIVATION A common weed that spreads easily and can be invasive. It does best in full sun and well-drained soil.

RELATED SPECIES Ribwort plantain (*P. lanceolata*) is another garden weed; *P. nivalis* is a compact species that suits rock gardens.

Aubretia
Aubrieta deltoidea

This evergreen perennial forms mounds which trail over rocks and walls. The purple to lilac flowers last from March to June, and Starlings and House Sparrows take early flowers for nesting.

HEIGHT 8–10cm (3–4in)
SPREAD 40–60cm (16–23in)

CULTIVATION Grows in well-drained soil in full sun. Cut back after flowering to maintain the compact mound.

RELATED SPECIES *A. x cultorum* 'J. S. Baker' bears purple, white-eyed flowers.

Starling

Fat hen
Chenopodium album

The seeds of this tall, annual weed attract several bird species throughout winter, either when on the plant or when dispersed on the ground.

HEIGHT 1m (3½ft) **SPREAD** 30cm (12in)

CULTIVATION Grows best in fertile soil but will also colonize bare ground. Sow seeds of the cultivated variety in spring. It flowers from June to October.

RELATED SPECIES Good King Henry (*C. bonus-henricus*) bears flower spikes.

Lemon balm
Melissa officinalis

A branching, herbaceous perennial of the mint family, grown for its lemon-scented leaves. Its seeds attract Goldfinches.

HEIGHT 80cm (31in) **SPREAD** 45cm (18in)

CULTIVATION Sow seed in autumn or spring. Plant in moist soil in partial sun. Can be grown from stem cuttings.

RELATED SPECIES *M. o.* 'All Gold' has yellow foliage. *M. o.* 'Aurea' has dark green and yellow variegated foliage.

Dandelion
Taraxacum officinale

This common and intrusive perennial herb thrives in lawns and herbaceous borders. The seedheads are a great attraction for finches and other birds.

HEIGHT 30cm (12in)
SPREAD 15cm (6in)

CULTIVATION An invasive weed that seeds freely. Leave seedheads uncut to attract birds.

RELATED SPECIES No cultivated varieties.

Sunflower
Helianthus annuus

This tall annual bears a single, large, daisy-like flower. The seeds are eaten by many species, including Long-tailed Tits and are a major constituent of proprietary birdfeeder mixes.

HEIGHT 3m (10ft) **SPREAD** 60cm (23in)

CULTIVATION Prefers full sun and well-drained soil, and requires staking to support the huge flowers. Hang cut seedheads for ready-made birdfeeders.

RELATED SPECIES There are a number of varieties, including dwarf forms; *H. a.* 'Teddy Bear' is suitable for containers; *H. x laetiflorus* and willow-leaved sunflower (*H. salicifolius*) suit wild gardens.

Long-tailed
Tit

Golden rod
Solidago virgaurea

A herbaceous perennial with small, yellow, daisy-like flowers, followed by heads of small hairy seeds which attract birds, such as Siskins.

HEIGHT 75cm (29in) **SPREAD** 45cm (18in)

CULTIVATION Grow in poor soil in sun or part-shade. Stake as necessary, and cut to the ground before the new growth starts. Self-seeds easily.

RELATED SPECIES *S.* 'Golden Wings' thrives in poor soil; Canadian golden rod (*S. canadensis*) has naturalized in many places.

Groundsel
Senecio vulgaris

This annual weed bears small yellow flowers throughout the year, followed by small globes of wind-blown seeds, which are eaten by finches.

HEIGHT 40cm (16in) **SPREAD** 10cm (4in)

CULTIVATION A weed that needs no cultivation and grows in any soil. It seeds freely and flourishes in flowerbeds. Cultivated varieties need moderately fertile soil in full sun.

RELATED SPECIES Cinererias, including *S. cinereria*, have silvery-green, felted leaves.

Michaelmas daisy
Aster novi-belgii

A tall, branching perennial introduced from North America. Clusters of violet flowers with yellow discs are produced in September and October. It attracts late insects and the seeds are eaten by Siskins.

HEIGHT 1m (3½ft)
SPREAD 50cm (20in)

CULTIVATION Prefers moist soil in sun. Propagate by dividing plants or as cuttings in spring or summer. Stake taller plants.

RELATED SPECIES *A. tradescantii* bears white flowers; *A. alpinus* is suitable for rock gardens.

Siskin

Yarrow (milfoil)
Achillea millefolium

This scented, perennial herb bears flat clusters of whitish flowers that develop into small seedheads. Birds are attracted to the seeds and to pollinating insects.

HEIGHT 60cm (23in)
SPREAD 60cm (23in)

CULTIVATION Prefers a sunny, dry site. Stake stems, especially in exposed places.

RELATED SPECIES *A. m.* 'Fire King' has red flowers.

Cornflower
Centaurea cyanus

Grown for its bright blue flowers, this is an annual herb that sometimes survives the winter. The seeds are eaten by Blue Tits and Greenfinches.

HEIGHT 1m (3½ft) **SPREAD** 30cm (12in)

CULTIVATION Sow in late summer or spring in well-drained soil with a sunny aspect. Ideal for naturalizing in grass.

RELATED SPECIES Greater knapweed (*C. scabiosa*) is a common perennial weed; perennial cornflower (*C. montana*) spreads vigorously.

Welted thistle
Carduus acanthoides

A biennial of hedges and verges, the thistle's purple flowers are visited by many insects, while in autumn, the seeds are eaten by many birds.

HEIGHT 1.2m (4ft)
SPREAD 50cm (20in)

CULTIVATION A weed that grows anywhere and easily self-seeds.

RELATED SPECIES Nodding or musk thistle (*C. nutans*) has red-purple flowers.

Observing garden birds

Even the smallest of urban gardens attracts a variety of birds. An understanding of what to look for will greatly enhance your enjoyment of these visitors, and knowing what basic equipment to use will help you explore their secret lives.

How to look

BIRDWATCHING CAN BEGIN at home. While it is exciting to look for birds in wild places, the elements of observation and identification are best learned in the familiar surroundings of the garden. And because you have some control over your garden environment, it is possible to conduct simple ecological studies that reveal birds' covert behaviours.

Home study

Your house is an ideal, ready-made hide. It is easy to watch birds at close range without disturbing them, especially if you position feeders close to windows. Proximity gives you a luxury rarely afforded in the field – the time and opportunity to examine plumage, bill shape, eye colour, and other details.

Brief observations can be made while you go about your everyday activities, but it is worth putting aside some time for "serious" garden birdwatching. Leave a pair of binoculars by the window, ready to be used when an unexpected bird turns up, or leave your telescope permanently trained on a busy birdfeeder.

When observing from within your house, try standing further back in the room; wary species, such as Sparrowhawks and crows, can be scared off by the slightest movement.

The garden is a good place for watching birds at close range; here, their everyday behaviour may be studied.

Learning how to identify birds is a goal in itself (see pages 80–81), but it is limited in the garden environment, where about a dozen or so common species account for the overwhelming majority of birds seen. It is worth observing birds in more detail, recording their behaviour throughout the day, and over the year.

Using a telescope in the garden gets you as close to wild birds as you are ever likely to be. Views at this range can be stunning and revealing.

A garden shed *or summer house makes a convenient hide to allow observation in remote corners of the garden.*

Ornithologists use numbered bird rings to record the local and migratory movements of birds. They may also monitor mating fidelity, nesting place, and life expectancy.

Investigating birds' private lives, and noting down changes in bird activity over time provides a means of understanding your garden as a wildlife habitat.

When studying bird behaviour, you should always ask yourself how and why? You may, for example, see a bird taking food from a feeder for the first time. It could be a Blackbird or a Dunnock (both of which normally feed on the ground) or perhaps a new visitor to the garden, such as a Nuthatch. You should note how it manages the new technique. Does it struggle to cling to the feeder or is it naturally acrobatic like a tit?

Trying to work out why a bird behaves in a certain way is more difficult; we can merely infer its motivation from watching its behaviour as carefully as possible. For example, Collared Doves sometimes perch in the rain

with one wing raised. This is the same action as is used for sunbathing, so we infer that this is rain-bathing and serves the same purpose as splashing in a bird-bath.

Identifying individuals

To study behaviour over time, it helps to be able to identify individual birds. They can sometimes be distinguished by details of plumage, anatomy, or chance damage. This way, you can begin to examine group dynamics, and the breeding behaviour of individual birds throughout the year. Professional ornithologists often identify individuals by attaching numbered metal or plastic rings to their legs, using colour combinations

BIRD DETECTIVES

A diligent birdwatcher looks at the ground as well as at the skies. Birds leave many traces that reveal something about their habits and their identities. Examining traces helps to build up a natural history of garden birds.

Feathers may be moulted or lost during an attack. If the feather has been moulted, wear on the vane is usually visible; if lost in an attack, it may be damaged.

Footprints in the snow or on mud reflect a bird's gait, revealing whether it walks or hops. They may also suggest what the bird was doing.

A post covered with droppings is likely to be a regular perch. It may be used as a song-post or a roost. Train your scope on the post, and wait for the visitor.

A cone in a rock or tree crevice is a sign of woodpecker or Nuthatch activity. Cones or nuts are wedged in before being hammered open by the birds.

Plucking posts are perches where birds of prey pluck and dismember their prey. They are worth checking regularly for recent activity.

KEEPING A DISTANCE

The basic rule of birdwatching is that the welfare of the birds comes first. Birds cope with everyday disturbance in the garden, but it is tempting to try to get too close to identify a rare species or move vegetation to peer into a bird's nest. The sitting parent may be driven off, but even if it sits tight, the disturbance may attract predators. It may be necessary to avoid part of the garden until the young birds leave the nest.

Birdsong and calls *are important clues to a bird's identity, especially when it is hidden among foliage. A tape recorder to assist your memory, or a CD recording of common birdsong can be good investments.*

Take detailed notes *as soon as possible. Do not trust your memory. Written records also allow you to compare these descriptions.*

that can be recognized from a distance. Ringing birds requires a special permit, but if you find rings on dead or injured birds, send the number and details of where, when, and how the bird was found, together with your address, to the address shown on the ring. Eventually, you will receive a history of the bird saying where and when it was ringed.

Making records

Use a notebook to record your observations: write down numbers of birds seen, what they were doing, details of plumage, and other identification tips. Descriptions of a bird's appearance and sound in your own words are invaluable, because they will mean far more to you than the generic descriptions given in bird books. Wherever possible, use annotated sketches to record characteristics (see below). It does not matter if you cannot draw well. Work fast, and try to make several sketches before the bird disappears from view. Remember that the size and shape of the bird and the relative sizes of its body parts can be as important as colours, but try also to note down the colours of the legs, bill, and any stripes around the eyes.

HOW TO SKETCH BIRDS

Concentrate on the outline of the head and body

① Begin your sketch with the bird's basic shape. Two ovals show the relative size and position of the head and body and also indicate the length of the neck. The position and length of the tail and legs are also indicated.

Use simple shapes

② Pencil in the bird's feather patterns, and annotate patches of colours. Carefully note down any eyestripes, cheek patches, wingbars, and so on. If time allows, make separate sketches of parts of the body to highlight any details that catch your eye.

Adjust the shape of the head and body as your sketch develops

Add body contours

Keep building detail for as long as the bird is in view

③ By now the bird should be identifiable. Pay attention to details of the head and wings. Make notes of behavioural characteristics, such as gait and flight pattern – they can be just as useful as shape and colour.

Add notes to the sketch

④ Refer to your sketch and notes to draw up a finished colour image. When it is complete, compare your picture with published illustrations and photos. Note how it differs, and remember to check these points next time you see the bird in the field.

A bird's songs and calls are also characteristic, but harder to record than physical attributes. Descriptions like "a high-pitched, clear warble" may not mean much on re-reading, but transcriptions like "*tuey*" or "*tsk-tsk-tsk*" may paint a better picture of the sound. Songs and calls are easiest to remember if they can be fitted to English phrases, like "teacher-teacher" for the Great Tit or "did-he-do-it" for the Song Thrush.

Analysing records

The simplest records are lists. These may be lists of species seen in the garden, or birds that have visited a particular feeder. By comparing lists week-by-week, it becomes possible to analyse what is happening in the garden. You can answer questions like: do some birds come into the garden at certain times of year? Do Song Thrush food preferences change from spring to autumn? Did the first Blackcap arrive before the last Redwing left?

If you keep a thorough account of the numbers of birds in the garden, you may be able to detect even very subtle changes in bird populations – for example, the arrival of immigrant Blackbirds and Chaffinches in autumn, which boost the local population.

Some birdwatchers simply keep their observations in the original notebooks, but transcribing notes into a permanent diary allows you to organize and analyse your data in more detail. If you are thinking of making serious records, an inexpensive database program for your computer is a worthwhile investment.

A systematic watch on a feeder may show that some birds prefer to feed at particular times of the day or that others always feed in flocks. Sometimes the patient observer is rewarded with the sight of an unusual visitor.

Studying the behaviour of nesting birds in your garden may be very rewarding. Site nest-boxes with a good line of vision to the house, so that you can watch in all weather conditions.

Broken snail shells on a rock or path indicate that it is an "anvil", where a Song Thrush smashes shells to get at the soft bodies. These anvils show which species of snails are caught and when thrushes turn to hunting them.

split, or perhaps other birds assist the parents. When the eggs have hatched, record the number of visits made by each parent to the nest. You could try to correlate breeding success with temperature and rainfall; form your own hypotheses, and use bird records from previous years to test out your ideas.

Ecological experiments

If observing and recording bird activity stimulates your interest in natural history, try devising a few simple ecological projects. When you next see a Blue Tit or Wren searching for food in the rough bark of a tree trunk, use a magnifying glass to see if you can find what it was eating. If a Coal Tit is flying off with whole peanuts from a feeder, try to find where it is hiding them. And keep a watch on Blackbirds and Wrens to find out where they roost at night.

Nesting is perhaps the most interesting and varied behaviour to observe and study in the garden. Try to see if it is the male or female parent that builds the nest and incubates the eggs. Perhaps the duties are

Nest investigations

In late autumn, when nests have been abandoned, they can be examined without disturbing birds. Try to identify the building materials used and look for differences in construction between species. Look inside nests for addled eggs or dead nestlings, piles of berries hoarded by mice, or even bumblebee nests. To avoid possible infection, wear protective gloves, and avoid inhaling dust from the nest material.

Taking part

Systematic recording of garden birds becomes even more interesting if it is linked with local or national surveys conducted by wildlife organisations. In Britain, the Royal Society for the Protection of Birds (RSPB)

Careful dissection of owl pellets (below) reveal what a owl has eaten. Skulls of small mammals and birds are easy to identify (left) but there may also be hard parts of insects' bodies.

Plant life can give valuable clues about bird activity. If birds perch regularly on a fence, they deposit seeds of their favoured food plants in their droppings. These may germinate to produce a natural and unique hedge or weed patch.

THE RSPB BIG GARDEN BIRDWATCH

Every year, during the last weekend of January, the RSPB holds its Big Garden Birdwatch in which people are encouraged to count birds in their gardens. In 2003, counts came in from an incredible 300,000 people. They showed that Starlings are the most numerous garden birds, with an average of five per garden, followed by House Sparrows, Blue Tits, and Blackbirds. The most widespread garden bird is the Blackbird, which was recorded in 93% of all gardens, followed by the Blue Tit (87%) and Robin (85%). Because the birds have been counted in the same way since 1979, it is possible to see changes in their abundance. Starlings have decreased by two-thirds and the House Sparrow by one-half in this period. These winter numbers are reflected in changes in the nesting population. Blue and Great Tits, Chaffinches, Greenfinches, Collared Doves, and Woodpigeons have become more abundant in gardens.

Counting the birds *visiting your garden will reveal fluctuations in numbers. For birds that feed in large flocks, such as Starlings, a hand counter is a useful tool.*

and the British Trust for Ornithology (BTO) run surveys that depend on garden birdwatchers and do not call for specialist knowledge. The analysis of data collected from thousands of gardens across the country helps to demonstrate changes in bird populations, and reveals details of their habits. The results are important for planning conservation programmes as well as increasing our understanding of bird life.

BIRD TIMETABLES

Recording the timing of annual events in a bird's life can reveal unexpected influences on its behaviour. For example, global warming can be detected by the earlier arrival of spring migrant birds: Chiffchaffs and Blackcaps reach Britain about three days earlier for every 1°C rise in temperature. To generate your own

bird calendar, simply record the first occurrence of a particular type of behaviour – arrival, nest-building, hatching of eggs, and so on – for a particular species, such as the Swallow (below). Compare the data you have collected over a number of years and try to explain any trends you observe.

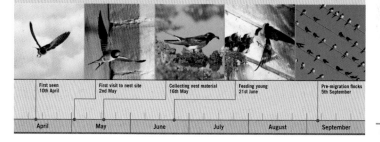

| First seen 10th April | First visit to nest site 2nd May | Collecting nest material 16th May | Feeding young 21st June | Pre-migration flocks 5th September |

April — May — June — July — August — September

Migration

BIRDS ARE ON THE MOVE throughout their lives. Every day, they may commute between their roosting and feeding grounds, and every year they may move between their summer and winter homes. Some birds migrate from a woodland breeding place in summer to a nearby garden for winter feeding, while others travel thousands of kilometres across continents.

Swallows summer *in Europe, gathering in small flocks in autumn before returning to their winter homes in Africa.*

Incredible journeys

Getting to know the movements of migrant species provides invaluable information about the birds in your garden. Every spring, we await the return of migrant birds from their winter in warmer countries. We watch for martins, Swallows, and Swifts darting overhead, and for warblers and flycatchers flitting amongst the newly opening foliage. Then, at the end of summer, these birds slip away again and we watch Redwings and Fieldfares arrive as they escape harsher climes.

Despite the huge expenditure of energy required to travel sometimes hundreds or thousands of kilometres, migration has clear benefits for many bird species.

Fieldfares are winter visitors *in southern and western Europe, where flocks of these large, colourful thrushes roam the countryside in search of food.*

These mainly revolve around the need to find good supplies of food, and to exploit sources of food that are seasonally abundant. It is wrong, however, to think that they are driven to migrate by hunger. Birds prepare for migration before food runs out, laying down fat to sustain them throughout their journey. They set off when wind and weather are favourable.

Most small birds migrate by night and are unlikely to be seen, while larger birds travel by day. Birds leave their breeding grounds in autumn in a fairly regular order. Swifts, and other birds that rely on a healthy supply of insects, depart early, while Swallows and martins, which manage to scrape a living even when flying insects are scarce, stay longer. A change to a vegetarian diet enables some warblers to delay departure for a few weeks.

Starlings are partial *migrants — some individuals migrate while others are resident all year round.*

In spring, birds hurry back to establish territories and make the most of the summer. Swallows spread northwards through Europe as temperatures increase, in a steady advance of about 40km (25 miles) per day, unless cold weather or a head-wind holds them up. Birds are sometimes seen when they stop to rest during migration. Many of these "birds of passage" are common birds, but birds from much further afield may turn up. This makes spring and autumn exciting times of the year.

In some winters, there is a sudden invasion of birds known as an "irruption". This occurs when the food supply fails in the birds' summer homes. Waxwings, for example, irrupt from northern European forests when rowan berry crops fail, and flocks appear in more southerly gardens to eat berries or windfall fruit.

ACCIDENTAL MIGRANTS

Migrating birds can sometimes become caught up in storms and be swept far off course, appearing thousands of kilometres from their normal routes. North American species, like this Golden-winged Warbler, migrate southwards along the east coast of North America. Caught by westerly gales, they can be carried across the Atlantic and deposited on European shores.

MIGRATION ROUTES

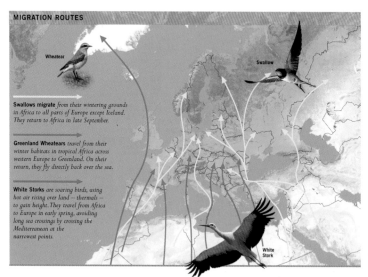

Wheatear

Swallow

Swallows migrate from their wintering grounds in Africa to all parts of Europe except Iceland. They return to Africa in late September.

Greenland Wheatears travel from their winter habitats in tropical Africa across western Europe to Greenland. On their return, they fly directly back over the sea.

White Storks are soaring birds, using hot air rising over land – thermals – to gain height. They travel from Africa to Europe in early spring, avoiding long sea crossings by crossing the Mediterranean at the narrowest points.

White Stork

The daily round

BIRDS ARE MOST NOTICEABLE when they are active – feeding, flying, singing, displaying, or fighting. They are especially visible in spring and summer when they must set up territories, find mates, build their nests, and tend their broods. Yet many birds spend a high proportion of their waking hours resting.

Cycles of activity

During a normal day outside the breeding season, a bird has two main activities. It has to feed, which it does in bouts through the day, and it must maintain its feathers in good condition by preening and bathing.

The first meal of a bird's day is particularly important because it helps replace the fat used up through the night to keep warm. However, birds are not in a hurry to start feeding in the morning. They may gather in nearby trees to preen and sing, but do not begin to feed until it is fully light. Some ornithologists think that birds delay their feeding activity because they cannot see well enough in the dim morning light to detect approaching predators, or locate food effectively.

Birds do not all become and remain active at the same times. Robins and Blackbirds, for example, are early risers, and are usually the last to disappear as

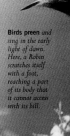

Birds preen and sing in the early light of dawn. Here, a Robin scratches itself with a foot, reaching a part of its body that it cannot access with its bill.

A Robin *contributes to the dawn chorus. A few minutes after waking up, it flies to a perch and sings for about an hour.*

Foraging takes up *a large part of a female Blackbird's day. She does not feed continuously, but takes part in other activities between bouts of eating.*

A Wren sunbathes *with its wings spread and body feathers raised. Sunbathing not only warms the body on a cold day, but is also thought to help with feather care.*

dusk gathers, while gulls and Starlings leave gardens early in the afternoon to return to their roosts when it is still light. In built-up areas that are illuminated by street and security lighting, birds may sing and sometimes even feed through the night.

Times of stress

A bird loses its free time twice during the year — once during the breeding season, when it struggles to feed its chicks and rear them to independence, and again in the winter, when its own survival becomes a struggle. Not only are there fewer daylight hours in the winter, but food is often in short supply, and extra rations are needed just to maintain body temperature in cold weather. As a result, small birds may have to spend most (if not all) of their daylight hours looking for food, and many leave their roosts before sunrise in an attempt to find additional feeding time.

This chart shows *how a male Nuthatch spends a spring day. Nearly two thirds of its time is spent looking for food. At this time of year, it also has to patrol its territory, singing and driving off other males.*

- Resting
- Singing
- Foraging
- Other
- Aggressive encounters
- Flying
- Preening

Keeping clean

When not feeding, birds devote much of their time to keeping their feathers in top condition; when feathers are damaged, insulation and waterproofing are impaired, and flight becomes more strenuous. The barbs that hold the feather vanes together become "unzipped" by daily wear and tear, and the bird must zip them back up using its bill. Preening consists of gently nibbling or stroking the feathers one at a time with the closed bill so that splits between the barbs are zipped up. The nibbling and rubbing also removes dirt and parasites (such as feather lice and mites) and arranges feathers back into position. At intervals during preening, the bird squeezes its bill against the preen gland at the base of its tail to collect preen oil, which it spreads in a thin film over the feathers; the oil is thought to kill bacteria and fungi.

Birds dislodge external parasites from their bodies by bathing; most will ruffle their feathers in a pond or puddle, but some indulge in dust baths or even "bathe" in the smoke from a chimney or fire.

After its bath *in a garden pond, this Green Woodpecker will fly to a safe perch and ruffle its feathers to settle them into place.*

Like other birds, *warblers set aside time every day for a thorough, systematic preen. The bill — in conjunction with scratching and fluffing movements — is used to arrange the feathers.*

Outside the nesting season, *Starlings fly in flocks to roost for the night. They also have day roosts where they preen between periods of foraging.*

Equipment

WATCHING BIRDS AT CLOSE QUARTERS is a special pleasure, and in the garden it is possible to get great views with the naked eye. However, a good pair of binoculars or a telescope bring you even closer to the action. It is also possible to make remarkably intimate photographs of garden birds with basic equipment.

Adjusting your eyepiece *settings according to the manufacturer's instructions ensures the crispest image.*

Choosing binoculars

Binoculars are an essential tool, especially when you get serious about your birdwatching. They do not enable you to see any further, but by magnifying what is already visible they allow you to identify and examine birds from a greater distance than with the naked eye. Binoculars come in many shapes and sizes. Generally, larger models give greater magnification, but magnifying power is not the only factor to bear in mind when choosing a pair to buy. You should also consider image brightness, build quality, ease of use, and, of course, price.

Comfort and magnification

The key specifications of a pair of binoculars are given by a pair of numbers – 10x40, for example. The first figure is the magnification, indicating how many times larger an object will appear when viewed. The second is the diameter of the objective lens; the larger this is,

Binoculars for use *in the garden should have a short minimum focus for close-up views. Check the closest focus before buying – models vary considerably.*

TYPES OF BINOCULARS

All binoculars use reflective prisms to extend the path of light, while retaining a compact body. There are two basic designs – roof prism (right) and the simpler, and cheaper porro prism (see below). Each design has its advantages.

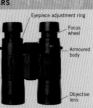

- Eyepiece adjustment ring
- Focus wheel
- Armoured body
- Objective lens

Traditional style binoculars *use a porro prism design. This simple optical arrangement is rugged and offers great value to the beginner. The widely separated objective lenses help to produce an excellent three-dimensional image.*

Waterproof optics, *a rubber-clad body, and retractable eyecups give these porro prism binoculars good all-weather performance. The lenses are made of low-dispersion glass to maintain colour accuracy. Coatings on the lenses minimize internal reflections.*

Compact models, *such as this 8x23 porro prism design, are highly portable and ergonomically designed for maximum comfort when held in one hand. The small objective lens, however, limits the brightness of the image.*

Roof prism binoculars *have a straight body. They are slender and compact, but the prisms more complicated than in porro prism binoculars, so the glass and manufacturing need to be of a higher quality, reflected in their higher price.*

Some binoculars can be fitted with an optional eyepiece that converts them into a short telescope. This rarely produces quality that matches the best purpose-built telescopes, but it is an affordable option for those wishing to get closer to birds.

Objective lens

Eyepiece attachment

Tilt control

Tripod

the brighter the image will seem. Ranges of 7 x 35 to 10 x 50 are ideal: higher magnifications may seem appealing but with a very narrow field of view they are hard to hold steady. Pay attention to comfort – the binoculars should fit well in your hands and be light enough to carry. When choosing binoculars, bear in mind that the focus wheel will be in constant use; you should be able to turn it effortlessly with a fingertip.

How to use binoculars

The first sign of a bird's presence is likely to be its call. Get its general bearings first by using your ears, then, facing the area, try to see the bird. The secret of keeping the bird in sight is to square yourself up to the target. Your whole body, including your feet, should turn to face the bird, and your whole head should tilt

The slightest jolt is magnified by binoculars. Leaning against a solid object helps to stabilize the image.

BINOCULARS AND GLASSES
People who wear spectacles often find that viewing through binoculars results in a poor image. This is because the eye is too far away from the binocular eyepiece and light can enter from the side. A raised finger or thumb helps block out this stray light, but the edges of the image may still appear blurred or dark. To avoid this problem, buy binoculars with eyepieces that are adjustable for spectacle wearers.

Normal eyesight   **Corrected for spectacles**

up to face the bird – not just your eyes. Now, keeping your head and body still, swing the binoculars up to your eyes, always keeping the bird fixed in view. You should find that you are looking straight at the bird.

Do not look down at your binoculars while lifting them up and then swing them around trying to find what you are looking for, because you are likely to lose the position of the bird. Wedge a finger against your forehead, or your thumb against your chin, for extra stability, or rest your arms against a window ledge or tree branch.

When walking outside, carry your binoculars on a strap around your neck. Do not keep them inside a case because they need to be ready for action at all times. When leaving a cool room to go out into warmer, more humid conditions, get your binoculars out of their case a few minutes before you need them. This reduces the degree of fogging that occurs as water condenses on the cold lenses.

Telescopes and tripods

Even closer views can be achieved with a telescope. Most models targeted at birdwatchers provide a magnification of about 30x or more; however, the observed object is magnified along with any

Digiscope view

vibrations or tremors caused by shaking hands. For this reason, telescopes need to be firmly supported on a tripod, bean bag, or clamp to be of practical value.

Many telescopes have a fixed focal length, but it is worth considering those fitted with zoom lenses, which provide more flexibility. In the past, a long focal length was achieved through long physical length, and

All scopes come equipped *with a screw bracket that allows them to be fixed to a standard camera tripod. Low-level viewing gives the greatest stability.*

Naked eye

Digital camera

Adapter

Objective lens

Tripod head

Digiscope equipment

Digiscoping *puts magnifications of up to 100x into the hands of amateurs equipped with a scope and a digital camera. Certain models are more suited to digiscoping than others.*

telescopes had to be made of several extendable sections for portability. Now, many modern telescopes use internal prisms to reduce length; some are very compact indeed.

As with binoculars, the brightness of the image depends, in part, on the diameter of the lens, so you will have to balance light intake with bulk. Special lenses, designated fluorite or ED, increase image brightness, but add to weight and cost.

Telescopes may be fitted with straight or angled eyepieces; the former are easier and more intuitive to "aim". Angled telescopes are far more comfortable to

use when mounted on a tripod, especially when keeping low to the ground; and a view of a bird is easier to share between people of different heights.

Observing with a telescope

Getting the most from a telescope takes a little practice. Lining it up with a bird presents the first challenge. As the instrument has a very narrow angle of view, the simplest, most effective technique is to look along the casing of the telescope to roughly align it with the bird, and only then to bring your eye to the eyepiece.

Always keep your eye directly in line with the eyepiece; if it is off-centre, the image you see will be vignetted or in soft focus. (This is harder than it sounds, especially if using a straight telescope fixed to a tripod.) Also, try keeping both eyes open; this will ease eye strain and you will be aware of other birds as they enter your peripheral field of vision.

CHOOSING TELESCOPES AND ACCESSORIES

Most birdwatchers favour angled, compact telescopes (right) over straight models. They do, however, take a little getting used to, because you do not look straight at the bird.

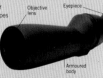

Objective lens

Eyepiece

Armoured body

Movable head

Telescoping leg sections

Rubber feet for grip on smooth surfaces

The ideal tripod *is lightweight, rigid, strong, portable, easy to set up, and tall enough for comfortable viewing. It has a "fluid head", which allows smooth movement with one control.*

Most telescopes *have changeable eyepieces. Wide-angled eyepieces of 20x to 30x are good for general use; 40x eyepieces are good for long-distance work, and zoom eyepieces give more versatility.*

Standard 30x eyepiece

Zoom eyepiece

MAGNIFICATION

Binoculars and telescopes magnify the image that you see with the naked eye, but will not improve the image on a dull or misty day. A standard pair of binoculars may magnify the image by eight times, while a telescope gives a far higher magnification of 30x or more. Too high a magnification, however, results in a blurred image unless the telescope can be held very steady.

Naked eye   8x   30x

Digiscoping

The widespread use of digital cameras and digital video cameras in recent years has put still higher magnifying power in the hands of the telescope user.

By attaching the zoom lens of a digital camera to the eyepiece of a telescope (see opposite), it is possible to achieve magnifications equivalent to those produced by a (very costly and cumbersome) 3,000mm lens on a conventional 35mm camera. The high-quality images produced by this technique, known as digiscoping, can be viewed and edited quickly.

A clamp is especially useful *for a permanent position in a hide. The telescope can be mounted quickly when needed in a hurry and the clamp provides a very firm base.*

Setting the shutter to a high speed (more than $\frac{1}{250}$ second) reduces the effects of camera shake. High shutter speeds also help to "freeze" the motion of birds in flight.

Changing the aperture (the diameter of the metal-bladed iris within the camera lens) affects the amount of light reaching the film. Together with shutter speed, this gives control over exposure.

A flashgun can illuminate a subject in low light or complete darkness, but is just as useful in daylight, when it can light birds in deep shade.

Even equipped with a long telephoto lens, you will need to get within a few metres of a bird to get a frame-filling shot. This will test your field skills. Sit-and-wait tactics often pay dividends.

Exposure controls

A camera records an image when light, focused by the lens, falls on to a film (or a CCD – the digital equivalent of film). The amount of light reaching the film must be carefully controlled to achieve the correct exposure; too much light results in pale, washed out pictures (overexposure); too little light produces dark, muddy images (underexposure). Many people are content to set their camera to automatic or "program" mode and allow its onboard computer to

Photographing birds

The key to capturing outstanding bird images is getting close. For this, you will need a telephoto lens (sometimes called a "long" lens), and a camera to which it can be fixed, or a digital camera with a long zoom range.

From the many film camera formats on offer, most bird photographers choose 35mm SLR cameras. "35mm" refers to the size of the film used in the camera, while "SLR" stands for Single Lens Reflex – meaning that you view the scene and take the photograph through one lens, so what you see in the viewfinder is (more or less) what appears in your photograph. SLR cameras are convenient because they have interchangeable lenses, so one camera body can take both wide-angle and telephoto pictures. Telephoto lenses favoured by bird photographers have focal lengths of 300 to 600mm (giving angles of view of 6° and 3°). They are capable of recording high-quality frame-filling images of birds; however, they are not only costly, but heavy and bulky.

For the photographic novice, a digital camera may be a better option. The images it produces can be viewed immediately, and, with no need for film and processing, its running costs are much lower.

FILM CAMERAS

35mm Single Lens Reflex cameras offer the best compromise between portability, affordability, and quality. Invest in a good long lens with a focal length of 300 or 500mm or a "long" zoom lens.

Camera body

Shutter release

Autofocus lens

Wide-angle lens

Zoom lens

A 24mm wide-angle lens and a medium-range zoom – say 35–105mm – plus a long telephoto will cover most photographic situations.

Pan and tilt head

Telescopic legs

A tripod is essential for preventing camera shake when using a long lens. Buy the heaviest and most sturdy that you can bear to carry.

Birds will approach *a fixed hide quite boldly. Mount your camera on a sturdy tripod, and train it on a nearby feeder or bird-table.*

sort out exposure and focus. In most situations this produces acceptable results, but experimenting with different exposure settings on your camera will help you make more creative images.

Making light work

It is worth assessing the "quality" of the light before pressing the shutter. For example, diffuse sunlight, filtered through thin cloud or patchy leaves, is ideal for capturing a naturalistic portrait of a bird. Morning and evening light illuminates a bird from the side, adding interest (and a golden colour cast) to your pictures, while overhead light in the middle of the day tends to be less flattering.

A zoom lens *on a digital camera may magnify an object 3x, while the "digital zoom" capability adds another 4x magnification. Total zoom capacity of 12x is good enough to make frame-filling pictures of birds.*

Direct sunlight produces dense shadows that can appear as ugly "black holes" in a photograph; firing a flashgun set to low power can help "fill in" these shadows to produce a more balanced image. Flash can also be used to "freeze" a bird in motion.

Setting a slower *shutter speed allows a bird's movement to "paint" the scene. Used creatively, blur may give atmosphere to an ordinary image.*

Setting a wide lens *aperture gives a shallow zone of crisp focus (depth of field). This effect can help to isolate a bird against a fussy background.*

The burst of light *from a flashgun lasts as little as one ten-thousandth of a second. It allows every feather to be seen in sharp relief.*

Bird profiles

Identification is an essential skill for any garden birdwatcher, and learning bird characteristics is a satisfying end in itself. The directory on the following pages profiles a number of the most common garden visitors.

Recognizing birds

Bird identification is a skill that can be honed by study and experience, but which can take a lifetime to master. Appearance and song give the most immediate clues to a bird's identity, but location, season, and habitat are also important factors to consider. In time, and with patience, you should be able to identify birds with ease.

A flash of white on the rump and wing of a Jay identifies it in flight.

Feathers are *arranged around well-defined feather tracts. It is useful to be familiar with the names of the main tracts.*

Nape
Crown or cap
Back
Greater coverts
Tertials
Secondaries
Shoulder patch (lesser coverts)
Median coverts
Primaries
Alula
Primary coverts
Tail
Flank
Belly
Under tail coverts
Vent

Brambling

Median coverts
Primaries
Greater coverts
Secondaries
Wingbar
Primary coverts
Rump
Tertials
Outer tail feathers

Brambling in flight

Reliable signs

Most species have "absolute" characters that will identify them – a Robin's red breast or the stumpy tail of a Wren, for example. However, birds rarely present themselves in textbook poses, and relying on a single characteristic to identify a bird can be unreliable. A bird's colour and plumage pattern may change over the course of a year and its size is difficult to judge in the absence of objects to provide a sense of scale. Shape is trickier still, because a bird can fluff or sleek its feathers, extend its neck, or spread its wings and tail to change its profile.

Rather than focusing on single characteristics, seasoned birdwatchers talk about the "jizz" of a bird, which is an amalgam of its physical appearance, behaviour, and personality. It allows them to identify birds just as we recognize

To assess a bird's size, it is useful to compare it to other, familiar species.

RELATIVE SIZES

Blue Tit
Chaffinch
Blackbird
Woodpigeon
Carrion Crow

50
40
30
20
10
0
cm

A Nightingale may *be hidden from sight in a tree but its identity is betrayed by its distinctive song.*

Cuckoos can sometimes *be mistaken for Sparrowhawks, but they winter in Africa, ruling them out for part of the year.*

our friends – from their walk, the way they hold their bodies, and other characteristic mannerisms.

Studying books and articles, and listening to birdsong on CD, will help familiarize you with a bird's features, behaviour, and sounds, but there is no substitute for observation in the field (or your garden). Soon, you will learn to differentiate the swooping flight pattern of a Swallow from the flickering, jerkier wingbeats of a House Martin, and the liquid cadence of a Willow Warbler from the staccato song of a Chiffchaff. Learning about plumage terminology (see opposite) is useful because it helps you compare your own observations, and notes with books, and allows you to share your findings with other enthusiasts.

Behaviour is an *excellent clue to identity, especially when details of plumage or anatomy cannot be seen. From afar, this Nuthatch can be distinguished from a Treecreeper because it is walking down a tree trunk (Treecreepers only walk upward).*

ABOUT THE BIRD PROFILES

The following pages describe 40 of the most common European garden birds, giving details of their size, shape, colour, voice, and behaviour. Distribution maps (see below for key) show the seasonal range of the species; the letters below the maps indicate the months during which the bird can be seen in the UK.

KEY

Summer distribution

Resident all year

Winter distribution

Seen on migration

Sparrowhawk
Accipiter nisus

PRIMARILY A BIRD of woodland margins, the Sparrowhawk may be seen in larger gardens that allow room for low, predatory flight; victims are snatched from perches or after a protracted chase. Mature females are larger than males, and often hunt small mammals.

Short, small head

Yellow bill with black tip

Dark grey-blue or brown upperparts

Barred orange underparts

Yellow legs

Broadly barred tail

Rather short, rounded wings

Soars with wings forward

LENGTH 28–40cm (11–16in)
WINGSPAN 60–80cm (23–31in)
VOICE Shrill, chattering *kek-kek-kek* usually near the nesting place.
EGGS One clutch of 4–6 grey-green eggs

in April–May.
REARING Female incubates eggs for 32–36 days, and is fed by the male; fledging is 24–30 days after hatching.
DIET Small birds such as sparrows and tits.

Collared Dove
Streptopelia decaocto

PREFERRING TO LIVE in towns and villages or near farms, the Collared Dove often resides in gardens, nesting in trees and hedges. The male advertises his territory with a dramatic display flight, and both parents perform "injury-feigning" displays – flapping their wings or limping across the ground – to lure predators from the nest.

Dark grey wingtips

Long, square-ended tail

Big, black eyes

Distinctive black-and-white collar

Red legs

Pale grey and brown plumage

LENGTH 31–33cm (12–13in)
WINGSPAN 47–55cm (18–21in)
VOICE Repeated monotonous *coo-COO-cook* and a nasal *whurr-whurr*.
EGGS 3–6 clutches

of two white eggs in March–November.
REARING Eggs are incubated for 14–18 days, fledging is 17 days after hatching.
DIET Seeds, leaves, buds, fruit, grain, bread, scraps.

Woodpigeon
Columba palumbus

A WILD AND SHY BIRD in the countryside, the Woodpigeon becomes tame in residential areas, and is a frequent visitor to garden bird-baths in summer. It takes off with loud, clattering wings when disturbed. It is distinguished from other pigeons by white, crescent-shaped patches on the midwing.

Grey back

White crescent across midwing

Black tail band

Pale yellow eye

Distinctive white neck patch

Reddish bill with a white patch at the base

Browner lower back

Warm pink breast

Dull red-pink legs

LENGTH 40–42cm (16in)
WINGSPAN 75–80cm (29–31in)
VOICE Plaintive *coo COO coo coo-coo*; nasal *gwurrrr* in flight.
EGGS Two or more clutches of two

white eggs from February–November.
REARING Eggs are incubated for 17 days by both sexes; fledging is 20–35 days after hatching.
DIET Leaves, berries, seeds, bread.

Great Spotted Woodpecker
Dendrocopos major

Vivid red patch on back of head

Black-and-white upperparts

Short, strong bill

White underparts

THE GREAT SPOTTED WOODPECKER is not always welcome in gardens, because it sometimes raids nest-boxes, eating eggs and young. The male has a crimson nape (lacking in the female); the juvenile bird has a red crown. They may be recognized by their fast, undulating, flapping and gliding flight. Outside the breeding season, it is rare to see more that one at a time at a bird-feeder.

Prominent, white shoulder patches

Red patch under tail

LENGTH 22–23cm (9in)
WINGSPAN 34–39cm (13–15in)
VOICE Loud *chick*; rapid drumming of the bill on a branch.
EGGS One clutch of 4–7 white eggs in

April–June.
REARING Eggs are incubated for 10–13 days by both sexes; fledging is 21 days after hatching.
DIET Insects, seeds, nuts, fruit, fungi, sap, fat.

Swift
Apus apus

No OTHER BIRD spends as much time in the air as the Swift. After nesting, a Swift may not land again until it returns to its nest the next spring, after mating on the wing. In flight, it has an arrow-shaped silhouette. Swifts rarely perch, but may cling to walls or rooftops.

Short bill, only just visible

Pale chin

Sharply pointed, scythe-shaped wings

Dark brown wings, tail, and body

Short, forked tail

J F M A M J J A S O N D

LENGTH 16–17cm (6–6½in)
WINGSPAN 42–48cm (16–19in)
VOICE Screaming *sree* from flocks; chirping when at the nest.
EGGS One brood of 2–3 white eggs in

May–July.
REARING Eggs are incubated for 18–22 days by both sexes; fledging is 35–56 days after hatching.
DIET Flying insects such as aphids, beetles, and midges.

House Martin
Delichon urbica

THE HOUSE MARTIN once occupied cliffs and rocky outcrops, but now more often nests under the eaves of houses. It can be seen perched on rooftops, at home in its mud-nest, or in large migratory flocks. In flight, House Martins reveal a bright white rump; this is duller on juveniles.

Brown-black wings

Blue-black upperparts

Bright white rump

White, feathered legs

White throat

Forked tail without streamers

J F M A M J J A S O N D

LENGTH 12cm (4½in)
WINGSPAN 26–29cm (10–11in)
VOICE Soft, twittering song; contact calls include quick, chirping notes.
EGGS 1–3 clutches of 2–5 white eggs from

late May–August.
REARING Eggs are incubated for 15 days by both sexes; fledging is 22–32 days after hatching.
DIET Small flying insects, including flies and aphids.

Swallow
Hirundo rustica

THE SWALLOW SPENDS THE WINTER in Africa, returning to nest in much of Europe and moving north as the air warms up. Before and after nesting, it roosts communally in reed beds and scrub, and occasionally in buildings. It flies with shallow wingbeats, often interspersed with graceful swoops, and glides as it hunts for flying insects. Long tail streamers provide great manoeuvrability.

Black eye and dark eye-ring

Shiny, very dark blue upperparts

Red forehead, chin, and throat

Long, narrow wings

Long tail streamers

White to pale buff underparts

Dark breast band

Forked tail

J F M A M J J A S O N D

LENGTH 17–19cm (6½–7½in)
WINGSPAN 32–35cm (12–14in)
VOICE Twittering song; calls with *swit-swit-swit.*
EGGS 2–3 clutches of 4–5 red-spotted, white eggs from

May–August.
REARING Female incubates eggs for 14–15 days; fledging is 19–21 days after hatching.
DIET Large flying insects, such as bees, moths, and butterflies.

Pied Wagtail
Motacilla alba

OFTEN FOUND IN URBAN AREAS, the Pied Wagtail visits gardens to feed, and roosts communally in warehouses, city trees, and other warm, safe sites in winter. The Pied Wagtail picks up food while walking, but also pursues moving insects with darting runs and jumps.

Distinctive white face

Black cap and nape

Black upperparts

White belly and white-and-grey flanks

White streaks on black wings

Long, black tail

J F M A M J J A S O N D

LENGTH 18cm (7in)
WINGSPAN 25–30cm (10–12in)
VOICE Loud, sharp *chisick* in flight; musical *chee-wee* in defence of territory.
EGGS Two clutches of 3–5 brown-freckled,

whitish eggs in April–June.
REARING Female incubates eggs for 14 days; fledging is 14 days after hatching.
DIET Insects, spiders, snails, seeds, bread, cheese, mealworms.

Dunnock
Prunella modularis

COMMON IN BRITISH GARDENS, the Dunnock is a shy woodland bird in continental Europe, and is easily overlooked because of its skulking habits. It keeps near cover, and spends much of its time under bushes. A large part of its day is spent hopping along the ground, pecking continuously.

Rich brown, streaked upperparts

Grey crown with brown streaks

Grey head, throat, and breast

Short, pointed bill

Dark brown tail

Grey-brown rump

Red-brown legs

LENGTH 14cm (5½in)
WINGSPAN 19–21cm (7½–8in)
VOICE Rapid warbling, similar to the song of a Wren; sharp, shrill *tseep*.
EGGS 2–3 clutches of 4–5 blue eggs in

April–July.
REARING Female incubates eggs for 14 days; fledging is 12 days after hatching.
DIET Small insects, spiders, snails, worms, seeds, peanut hearts, oatmeal.

J F M A M J J A S O N D

Wren
Troglodytes troglodytes

THE TINY WREN IS SECRETIVE in its habits and prefers to keep to dense undergrowth. When in the open, it scurries like a mouse along the tops of fences and the edges of walls. Its powerful voice belies its tiny size; the female's scolding *chit* calls of alarm are a common sound in the garden. The Wren generally feeds on and near the ground but, amazingly, has also been known to catch tadpoles and goldfish.

Brown wings with dark bars

Pale stripe over eye

Rounded wings

Warm brown upperparts

Short tail, often cocked

Light brown legs

LENGTH 9–10cm (3½–4in)
WINGSPAN 13–17cm (5–6½in)
VOICE Shrill, trilling song; dry, rattling *tick-tick-tick*; rolling *churr*.
EGGS Two clutches of 5–6, usually

whitish eggs in April–July.
REARING Female incubates eggs for 16–17 days; fledging is 16–17 days after hatching.
DIET Small insects, mealworms, cheese.

J F M A M J J A S O N D

Robin
Erithacus rubecula

THE ROBIN'S NATURAL HABITAT of forest with a layer of undergrowth is mimicked by the hedges, shrubs, and trees of the British landscape; in other parts of Europe, the Robin is a shy woodland bird. It defends its territory fiercely, singing and fluffing out its characteristic red breast.

Warm brown tail

Olive-brown upperparts

Orange-red chin and throat

Large head

Large, black eye

Soft, blue-grey sides of neck and chest

Squat, round body

Long, thin, brown legs

Dull, buff underparts

LENGTH 14cm (5½in)
WINGSPAN 20–22cm (8–9in)
VOICE Bursts of liquid warbling; alarm calls are a thin *tseeee* and a repeated *tic*.
EGGS 2–3 broods of 5–6 red-speckled,

white, or bluish eggs from April–June.
REARING Female incubates eggs for 14 days; fledging is 13–14 days after hatching.
DIET Invertebrates, bread, mealworms, meat, potatoes, fat.

J F M A M J J A S O N D

Blackbird
Turdus merula

AS WOODLAND HABITATS have disappeared, mature gardens have become havens for the Blackbird, which forages through leaf litter. The adult male is easily identified by its stark, black plumage; the female is dark brown, with mottling on the throat and chest, and the juvenile is similar, but with a dark bill.

Uniformly black plumage

Yellow-orange eye-ring

Bright yellow bill

Plump, round body

Dark brown legs

Long, black tail

Slightly paler wingtips, visible from below

LENGTH 24–25cm (9–10in)
WINGSPAN 34–38cm (13–15in)
VOICE Warbling song; subdued *pook-pook*; hysterical rattle.
EGGS 2–4 clutches of 3–5 brown-freckled,

greenish-blue eggs from March–July.
REARING Female incubates eggs for 13 days; fledging is 13–14 days after hatching.
DIET Worms, insects, fruit, scraps, seeds.

J F M A M J J A S O N D

Song Thrush
Turdus philomelos

A RATHER SHY GARDEN VISITOR, the Song Thrush is more often seen feeding on the lawn and in flowerbeds than at the bird-table. It is distinguishable from the larger Mistle Thrush by the spots on its breast, which are shaped like upside-down hearts, and its direct rather than undulating flight.

Pale eye-ring
Medium brown upperparts
Black-brown spots
Buff underside with white belly
Heavily spotted underparts
Pale orange patch under wing

LENGTH 23cm (9in)
WINGSPAN 33–36cm (13–14in)
VOICE Fluting, musical song with repeated phrases; short *tick*; rattle of alarm.
EGGS 2–3 clutches of 4–6 blue eggs from March–August.
REARING Female incubates eggs for 13–14 days; fledging is 13 days after hatching.
DIET Fruit, small invertebrates, fat, sultanas, scraps.

J F M A M J J A S O N D

Mistle Thrush
Turdus viscivorus

NAMED AFTER ONE of its favourite foods – mistletoe berries – the Mistle Thrush is one of the largest European thrushes. It breeds widely across Europe, but it is never abundant. It often occupies larger gardens with tall trees that provide high song-posts, from which the male delivers its far-carrying, ringing song.

Pale patch around large, dark eye
Grey-brown upperparts
Grey wings
Dark, wedge-shaped spots on white underparts
Pale brown legs
Bright, white underwings

LENGTH 27cm (11in)
WINGSPAN 42–48cm (16–19in)
VOICE Powerful *tee-tor-tee-tor-tee* song; harsh and rattling calls.
EGGS Two clutches of four speckled, whitish eggs in late February–June.
REARING Female incubates eggs for 12–15 days; fledging is 12–15 days after hatching.
DIET Berries, insects, worms, bread, apples.

J F M A M J J A S O N D

Redwing
Turdus iliacus

SPENDING ITS SUMMERS in northern Europe, the Redwing migrates to southern and western Europe as conditions deteriorate. It is seen mainly on farmland, but visits gardens in cold weather to search for crops of berries – a flock can strip a tree of berries in a few hours.

Pale stripe above eye
Brown cheeks
Brown back
Pale breast with dark brown streaks
Rust red patch on flanks
Red-brown underwings
White under tail

LENGTH 21cm (8in)
WINGSPAN 33–35cm (13–14in)
VOICE The call, often given in flight, is a soft, lisping *see-ip*.
EGGS Two clutches of 4–6 red-brown speckled, pale blue eggs in May–June.
REARING Female incubates eggs for 12–13 days; fledging is 10 days after hatching.
DIET Insects, snails, slugs, earthworms, berries, apples.

J F M A M J J A S O N D

Fieldfare
Turdus pilaris

THE LONGTAILED FIELDFARE is a northern species that has colonized central Europe over the last 50 years. It forms large, nomadic feeding flocks, often mixed with Redwings. When in flight, its white underwing patches are a useful feature for identification.

Bright white underwing
Blue-grey head
Grey rump
Yellow bill
Chestnut brown back
Pale golden chest with dark streaks
Long, black tail

LENGTH 27cm (11in)
WINGSPAN 39–42cm (15–16in)
VOICE Chuckles and whistles with *chack* notes; harsh *chack-chack-chack*.
EGGS 1–2 clutches of 4–6 red-speckled, pale blue eggs from May–July.
REARING Female incubates eggs for 13–14 days; fledging is 14 days after hatching.
DIET Insects, seed, earthworms, fruit.

J F M A M J J A S O N D

Blackcap
Sylvia atricapilla

THE BLACKCAP DELIVERS its remarkable song from deep within the foliage of bushes and trees. It chooses territories with shrubby undergrowth and tall trees for feeding and perching; it may nest in mature gardens. The male has the characteristic black cap, while the female has a reddish-brown cap.

Grey-brown upperparts

Black cap

Plain, grey wings

Grey face and throat

Short grey tail with no white edges

Pale grey underparts

J F M A M J J A S O N D

LENGTH 13cm (5in)
WINGSPAN 20–23cm (8–9in)
VOICE Bright, pure notes with a "rippling" quality, often with an increase in volume.
EGGS 1–2 clutches of 4–6 buff-coloured

eggs with brown marks in April–June.
REARING Eggs are incubated for 10–16 days by both sexes; fledging is 10–14 days after hatching.
DIET Insects, nectar, fruit, kitchen scraps.

Garden Warbler
Sylvia borin

THE GARDEN WARBLER is a woodland bird and its presence in open woods with a layer of shrubs suggests that it ought to be found in mature gardens, but it is shy and does not tolerate disturbance, and garden visits are confined to passing migrants in spring and wandering juveniles in late summer.

Delicate, pale eye-ring

Plain brown upperparts

Short, strong bill

Pale neck patch

Brown wings

Buff underparts

Slightly darker brown wings

J F M A M J J A S O N D

LENGTH 14cm (5½in)
WINGSPAN 20–24cm (8–9in)
VOICE Song is similar to a Blackcap's; soft *tchak*; low *churrr*.
EGGS 1–2 clutches of 4–5 white, pink, or green eggs with

brown, purple, or olive markings in May–July.
REARING Eggs are incubated for 11–12 days by both sexes; fledging is usually 10 days after hatching.
DIET Insects, fruit, seeds.

Chiffchaff
Phylloscopus collybita

MANY CHIFFCHAFFS are migrants, spending the winter in Africa or southern Europe and returning to breed in Europe. When perched, the Chiffchaff continually bobs its tail and flicks its wings, and it can often be seen launching from a twig to catch flying insects.

Pale line over eye

Olive-brown upperparts

Dark eyes with pale eye-ring

Thin bill

Short, brown, rounded wings

Dull, pale yellow underparts

Dark brown or black legs

J F M A M J J A S O N D

LENGTH 10–11cm (4–4½in)
WINGSPAN 15–21cm (6–8in)
VOICE Hesitant *chiff-chaff-chiff-chiff* notes; calls with a loud *hweet*.
EGGS 1–2 clutches of 4–7 white eggs with

a few purplish marks in May–July.
REARING Female incubates eggs for 13–15 days; fledging is 14–16 days after hatching.
DIET Insects, fruits, berries.

Goldcrest
Regulus regulus

THE SMALLEST EUROPEAN BIRD, the Goldcrest lives almost entirely in conifer trees or nearby deciduous trees, rarely venturing down to the ground. Often difficult to see, its presence may be given away by its distinctive song. It is remarkably tolerant of human spectators.

Bold, yellow crest bordered with black

Large, black eyes

Two white wingbars

Paler, buff-green underparts

Dark wings

J F M A M J J A S O N D

LENGTH 9cm (3½in)
WINGSPAN 13–16cm (5–6in)
VOICE Thin, twittering *twedly-twedly-twedly-twiddledidee*; thin *see-see*.
EGGS Two clutches of 7–10 brown-spotted,

white or buff eggs in May–July.
REARING Female incubates eggs for 14–17 days; fledging is 16–21 days after hatching.
DIET Spiders, insects, bird cake, fat.

Spotted Flycatcher
Muscicapa striata

Fine, black streaks on crown

Grey-brown upperparts

Pale underparts

Dark legs

Long, brown tail

Long, brown wings

A SUMMER VISITOR to most of Europe, the Spotted Flycatcher inhabits gardens that provide perches for hunting, cover for nesting, and water for drinking and bathing. It flies out from a perch to seize flying insects in its bill while briefly hovering, before returning to its perch.

J F M A M J J A S O N D

LENGTH 14cm (5½in)
WINGSPAN 23–25cm (9–10in)
VOICE Song is a quiet, weak warble; call is a loud, thin see.
EGGS 1–2 clutches of 4–5 brown-spotted, greenish eggs in

May–July.
REARING Female incubates eggs for 12–14 days; fledging is 12–16 days after hatching.
DIET Flies, aphids, wasps, bees, butterflies.

Long-tailed Tit
Aegithalos caudatus

WITH ITS LONG TAIL and tiny body, the Long-Tailed Tit is an unmistakeable garden bird. In summer, it can be seen in family parties; outside the breeding season, they form larger feeding flocks. Juveniles lack the pink markings of the adult and have shorter tails, brown backs, and more grey on the head.

Very long, slender tail

Black band above eye

Dark, rounded wings

Pinkish-white underparts

Black tail with white edges

J F M A M J J A S O N D

LENGTH 14cm (5½in)
WINGSPAN 16–19cm (6–7½in)
VOICE Twittering trill; sharp tsirrup; high-pitched, repeated zee; short pit.
EGGS One clutch of 8–12 reddish-

freckled, white eggs in April–June.
REARING Female incubates eggs for 14–18 days; fledging is 14–18 days after hatching.
DIET Small insects, fat, meat, peanuts.

Coal Tit
Parus ater

Black head with white patch on the nape

Striking, white cheeks

Short, grey tail

Two white wingbars

Bold head pattern

Large, black bib

COAL TITS NEST and feed in the branches of conifers, and their presence in gardens has been increased by the fashion for planting conifer trees and hedges. Identified by its black bib and white nape patch, the Coal Tit is often seen at feeders in autumn; it takes the seeds to eat at leisure in the shelter of nearby foliage, or stores them for later consumption.

J F M A M J J A S O N D

LENGTH 11–12cm (4½in)
WINGSPAN 17–21cm (6½–8in)
VOICE Bright, high-pitched pee-choo pee-choo, tsee-tsee.
EGGS 1–2 clutches of 7–12 reddish-

spotted, white eggs in April–June.
REARING Female incubates eggs for 14–16 days; fledging is 18–20 days after hatching.
DIET Insects, seeds, peanuts, fat.

Blue Tit
Parus caeruleus

THE LIVELY BLUE TIT is credited with great intelligence, partly because of its ability to find new sources of food and the dexterity of foot and bill when feeding, but also because of its ability to learn from other birds by imitation. The male generally has brighter colouring than the female; juvenile birds have yellower cheeks and greenish rather than bright blue caps.

Blue wings with distinct white bars

Bright blue cap

Short bill

Black stripe across eye

Yellow underparts

Blue tail

J F M A M J J A S O N D

LENGTH 11cm (4½in)
WINGSPAN 17–20cm (6½–8in)
VOICE Tsee-tsee-tsu-hu-hu-hu; quick tsee; harsh tsee-tsee-sit; scolding churr.
EGGS Usually one clutch of 7–12

reddish flecked, white eggs in April–May.
REARING Female incubates eggs for 12–15 days; fledging is 16–22 days after hatching.
DIET Insects, seeds, fruit, meat.

Great Tit
Parus major

LARGER THAN THE OTHER TITS, the Great Tit is not as agile, and spends more of its time feeding on or near the ground. It is easily told apart from other tits by the distinctive black stripe on its underside, slightly narrower in the female. These vocal birds have a wide "vocabulary" and can recognize each other's songs.

Black cap, collar, and throat

White cheeks

Yellow-green back

Yellow underparts

Blue-grey tail

White wingbar on blue-grey wing

LENGTH 14cm (5½in)
WINGSPAN 22–25cm (9–10in)
VOICE Song is varied; calls include a familiar *tea-cher, tea-cher.*
EGGS 1–2 clutches of 5–12 reddish-spotted, white eggs

in April–June.
REARING Female incubates eggs for 12–15 days; fledging is 16–22 days after hatching.
DIET Seeds, fruit, insects, peanuts, fat, scraps.

JFMAMJJASOND

Marsh/Willow Tit
Parus palustris / Parus montanus

FOUND IN GARDENS with mature deciduous trees or near woodland, it is difficult to tell the Marsh Tit (*Parus palustris*) and the Willow Tit (*P. montanus*) apart, unless you hear their calls. The Marsh Tit is a woodland bird, while the Willow Tit prefers willows and birch on marshy ground.

Glossy, black cap

Black bib

Grey-brown upperparts

Pale grey underparts

Rounded wings

Marsh Tit

LENGTH 11–12cm (4½in)
WINGSPAN 18–19cm (7–7½in)
VOICE Marsh: *pitchou-pitchou.* Willow: *chay-chay-chay;* thin *zi-zi.*
EGGS 1–2 clutches of 6–9 white eggs with a

few red-brown spots in April–June.
REARING Female incubates eggs for 13–15 days; fledging is 17–20 days after hatching.
DIET Insects, seeds, berries, nuts, scraps.

JFMAMJJASOND

Nuthatch
Sitta europaea

Bold, black stripe through eye

Orange-buff underparts

THE NUTHATCH DOES NOT travel far and only comes into gardens near mature woodland, although it may nest in gardens with large trees. It has a pointed shape due to its long head and long bill, which it uses to hammer nuts open, making a tapping noise like a woodpecker.

Grey-blue upperparts

Round, grey wings

Short, square tail

Short bill

LENGTH 14cm (5½in)
WINGSPAN 16–18cm (6–7in)
VOICE Song is a rapid, trilling *chi-chi-chi;* call is a ringing *chit-chit.*
EGGS 1–2 clutches of 6–9 reddish-spotted white eggs

in April–May.
REARING Female incubates eggs for 14–15 days; fledging is 23–25 days after hatching.
DIET Spiders, insects, sunflower seeds, nuts, fat, bird cake.

JFMAMJJASOND

Treecreeper
Certhia familiaris

THE TREECREEPER is a brown, long-tailed bird that runs up tree trunks and out along branches, in a mouse-like manner. It then flies down to the base of the next tree and works its way up again. Unlike Nuthatches and tits, it does not hang head-down, and only hops upwards.

White stripe above eye

Long, curved bill

Streaked brown upperparts

Pale brown legs

White underparts

Long, rounded wings

Long tail

LENGTH 13cm (5in)
WINGSPAN 18–21cm (7–8in)
VOICE Song is a high, thin *see-see-see-sissi-sooee.*
EGGS 1–2 clutches of 5–7 brown-spotted, white eggs in

April–June.
REARING Female incubates eggs for 12–20 days; fledging is 13–17 days after hatching.
DIET Insects, spiders, small seeds, fat, peanuts, porridge.

JFMAMJJASOND

Jackdaw
Corvus monedula

A SOCIABLE BIRD, the Jackdaw can be seen in many suburban areas, where it nests in buildings and old trees. It hunts for insects in trees, but mainly forages for food on the ground or scavenges from rubbish bins. It is easily identified by its sharp *tchak* call, from which it gets its name.

Grey nape and cheeks

Black crown with a purple sheen

Pale grey eye

Dark, grey-black plumage

Black legs

Dark wings

LENGTH 33–34cm (13in)
WINGSPAN 67–74cm (26–29in)
VOICE Song is a variable medley that includes *tchak* calls.
EGGS One clutch of 4–6 spotted, pale blue eggs in April–May.
REARING Female incubates eggs for 17–18 days; fledging is 28–36 days after hatching.
DIET Cereals, fruit, insects, fat, carrion.

J F M A M J J A S O N D

Jay
Garrulus glandarius

THE UNMISTAKABLE JAY is a regular visitor to rural and suburban gardens and urban parks, preferring places where there are plenty of mature trees. It gives away its presence by its harsh, screeching cries, or is briefly seen as it flaps jerkily and heavily across clearings on broad wings.

Domed head

Bold, black moustache

White rump

Pale pink to grey-brown upperparts

Striking, blue panel on wing

White wing patch

Black tail

LENGTH 34–35cm (13–14in)
WINGSPAN 52–58cm (20–23in)
VOICE Rasping *krar*, mimics other birds.
EGGS One clutch of 3–6 brown-flecked, greenish eggs in April–June.
REARING Female incubates eggs for 16–17 days; fledging is 21–22 days after hatching.
DIET Acorns, seeds, fruit, insects, carrion, scraps, peanuts.

J F M A M J J A S O N D

Magpie
Pica pica

COMMON IN THE COUNTRYSIDE, the Magpie is also highly successful in urban areas. It remains in gardens year round; indeed few individuals stray more than a few kilometres from where they are hatched. Agile on the ground, the Magpie moves with a distinctive high-stepping walk interspersed with brisk jumps.

Prominent shoulder patch

Black breast

White belly (appears dirty on young birds)

Black wings with blue-green sheen

Broad, rounded wings

White wingtips with black streaks

Long, dark, iridescent tail

Black head and back

LENGTH 44–46cm (17–18in)
WINGSPAN 52–60cm (20–23in)
VOICE Harsh *kyack*; repeated *shak-shak-shak*.
EGGS One clutch of 3–9 speckled, greenish eggs in March–April.
REARING Female incubates eggs for 18 days; fledging is 24–30 days after hatching.
DIET Insects, seeds, fruit, bread, meat.

J F M A M J J A S O N D

Starling
Sturnus vulgaris

AT CLOSE RANGE, the Starling's plumage is surprisingly beautiful: glossy, blackish feathers reveal an iridescent sheen of metallic hues. It possesses a voracious appetite and will often clear a bird-table before others can claim their share. Outside the breeding season, Starlings swarm each evening, circling in the air with great precision.

Pointed, yellow bill turns brown in winter

Short, square-ended tail

Dark brown eyes

Triangular wings

Black plumage with a glossy green and purple sheen

Reddish-brown legs

LENGTH 21cm (8in)
WINGSPAN 37–42cm (14–16in)
VOICE Rattles, squeaks, and whistles; mimicked calls of other species.
EGGS 1–2 clutches of 4–6 pale blue eggs in March–April.
REARING Female incubates eggs for 11–15 days; fledging is 21 days after hatching.
DIET Invertebrates, bread, scraps, nuts, hanging bones.

J F M A M J J A S O N D

House Sparrow
Passer domesticus

THROUGH SUCCESSFUL EXPLOITATION of human settlements for shelter and food, the House Sparrow has been able to colonize many parts of the world. However, numbers have declined across Europe, possibly due to a lack of food sources vital for nestling survival.

Brown upperparts streaked with black

Grey cap

Bold, black bib

Pale grey underside

White wingbars

Grey, square-ended tail

Broad wings

J F M A M J J A S O N D

LENGTH 14cm (5½in)
WINGSPAN 20–22cm (8–9in)
VOICE Variety of *cheep* and *chirp* calls.
EGGS 2–3 clutches of 3–5 brown-blotched, white eggs in April–August.

REARING Eggs are incubated for 11–14 days by both sexes; fledging is 11–19 days after hatching.
DIET Seeds, scraps, and peanuts; nestlings are fed on insects.

Tree Sparrow
Passer montanus

FORMING LOOSE COLONIES in farmland, parks, and suburban fringes, the Tree Sparrow is very like the House Sparrow, but its crown lacks the grey centre, and it has a black spot on the white cheek. Within the last 30 years, its numbers have dropped by over 90 per cent.

Prominent black spot on white cheeks

White collar

Plain brown cap

Black bib

Pale, white-buff underparts

Short, brown tail

Brown back streaked with black

Two white wingbars

J F M A M J J A S O N D

LENGTH 14cm (5½in)
WINGSPAN 20–22cm (8–9in)
VOICE Basic *tchurp* note; in flight, the flock keeps in contact with rapid *tick* notes.
EGGS 1–3 clutches of 2–7 pale grey eggs

with brown marks in April–July.
REARING Eggs are incubated for 11–14 days by both sexes; fledging is 15–20 days after hatching.
DIET Seeds, bread; insects for nestlings.

Chaffinch
Fringilla coelebs

PRIMARILY A WOODLAND BIRD, the Chaffinch is also common in areas that have tall trees and prominent perches. The olive-brown female is less colourful than the male, but has similar white wingbars and tail edges. The Chaffinch has a broad bill with sharp edges, perfect for removing the husks from seeds.

Small, sharp bill

Blue-grey crown

Pinkish underside

Brown back

Dark wings

Olive-green rump

Long, dark tail

Striking white tail edges

Bright white wingbars

J F M A M J J A S O N D

LENGTH 15cm (6in)
WINGSPAN 25–28cm (10–11in)
VOICE *Chitp-chip-chip-chuwee-chuwee-tissichooee*, sharp *chink-chink*.
EGGS 1–2 clutches of 4–5 purple-

marked, blue eggs in May–June.
REARING Female incubates for 12–14 days; fledging is 11–18 days after hatching.
DIET Seeds, spiders, insects, peanuts.

Redpoll
Carduelis flammea

NAMED AFTER THE CRIMSON PATCH on its head, the Redpoll lives in open woodland, heaths, hedgerows, and young conifer plantations. It can be seen feeding at the tops of trees; it is more likely to feed in gardens if they have silver birch trees or wild areas.

Dark brown tail

Red forehead

Black chin

Pale brown, streaked upperparts

Two pale wingbars

Pinkish breast

Pale, streaked underparts

J F M A M J J A S O N D

LENGTH 11–15cm (4½–6in)
WINGSPAN 20–25cm (8–10in)
VOICE Staccato twittering with a *cha-cha-cha-charr*.
EGGS Two clutches of 4–6 bluish eggs

with reddish-brown specks in May–June.
REARING Female incubates eggs for 10–12 days; fledging is 9–14 days after hatching.
DIET Seeds, sunflower hearts, insects.

Greenfinch
Carduelis chloris

ORIGINALLY RATHER A SHY BIRD, the Greenfinch adapted well to garden life, and gradually colonized towns and cities over the last century. Gangs of Greenfinches can be seen in most bird-friendly gardens, foraging on the ground under feeders.

Pale flesh-coloured bill

Apple-green plumage

Green-yellow underparts

Bold yellow patch

Pale pink legs

Grey wings

Dark tail with yellow edges

LENGTH 15cm (6in)
WINGSPAN 25–27cm (10–11in)
VOICE Medley of notes ending in a loud wheeze; *chi-chi-chi-chi*; rasping *sweee*.
EGGS 1–3 clutches of 4–6 red-spotted, white eggs in April–June.
REARING Female incubates eggs for 12–14 days; fledging is 14–15 days after hatching.
DIET Weed, tree, and fruit seeds, peanuts.

J F M A M J J A S O N D

Goldfinch
Carduelis carduelis

PART OF THE Goldfinch population winters in its breeding range, part in southern Europe. Its tweezer-like bill is the ideal tool for extracting seeds; seedheads left on plants, and patches of weeds are the initial attractions in a garden for a hungry Goldfinch.

Bold, red face markings

Pale, pointed bill

Brown back

Sandy brown breast

Black, white, and yellow wings

White belly

Slightly forked tail

Broad, yellow bar

LENGTH 13cm (5in)
WINGSPAN 21–25cm (8–10in)
VOICE Call is a liquid *swift-witt-witt*; song is a musical twittering.
EGGS 1–3 clutches of 5–6 red-freckled, white eggs in May–August.
REARING Female incubates eggs for 11–12 days; fledging is 13–18 days after hatching.
DIET Insects, wild seeds, nyjer seeds, sunflower hearts.

J F M A M J J A S O N D

Siskin
Carduelis spinus

THE SPREAD OF CONIFER PLANTING has increased the Siskin's breeding range throughout Europe. It is a small finch with a markedly forked tail and clues to the acrobatic habits of a tit. In flight, the yellow bars on its wings and on the side of its tail are obvious.

Yellow-green back

Black cap

Black wings

Bold, yellow wingbar

Yellow rump

White belly

LENGTH 12cm (4½in)
WINGSPAN 20–23cm (8–9in)
VOICE *Tsooee* on the wing; sweet twittering culminating in a wheeze.
EGGS 1–2 clutches of 4–5 red-streaked, pale blue eggs in April–July.
REARING Female incubates eggs for 12–13 days; fledging is 13–15 days after hatching.
DIET Seeds, insects, peanuts, fat.

J F M A M J J A S O N D

Bullfinch
Pyrrhula pyrrhula

DESPITE ITS COLOURFUL PLUMAGE, the Bullfinch can pass unnoticed in thick foliage; the best clues to its presence are often its soft, whistled calls. The Bullfinch may feed on clover and dandelions in the lawn, very occasionally visiting a garden feeding station.

Bold, black cap and chin

Grey back

Short, black bill

Red-pink underparts

Dark wings with white wingbar

White rump

Short, dark legs

Black tail

LENGTH 15cm (6in)
WINGSPAN 22–26cm (9–10in)
VOICE Song is a quiet warbling; call is a whistling *deu-deu*.
EGGS Two clutches of 4–5 purple-streaked, green-blue eggs in May–June.
REARING Female incubates eggs for 12–14 days; fledging is 14–16 days after hatching.
DIET Seeds, buds, insects, peanuts, sunflower hearts.

J F M A M J J A S O N D

Glossary

Adult A fully mature bird, which is able to breed and is in its final plumage that no longer changes pattern with age

Barred With marks that cross the body, wings, or tail

Behaviour How a bird moves, calls, sings, nests, and carries out all aspects of its life, in a manner that is more or less characteristic of its species

Breeding plumage An imprecise but useful general term; usually refers to the plumage worn when birds display and pair

Brood Young produced from a single clutch of eggs, and incubated together

Call Vocal sound, often characteristic of a single species, communicating a variety of messages

Clutch A group of eggs in a single nest, usually laid by one female, and incubated together

Colony A group of nests of a social species that has some social function

Covert A small feather in a well-defined tract on the wing or at the base of the tail, covering the base of the larger flight feathers

Dabble To feed in shallow water by sieving water and food through comb-like filters in the bill, hence "dabbling duck"

Declining Of a population undergoing a steady reduction over a period of years

Display Ritualized, showy behaviour that is used in courtship and/or by a bird claiming a territory; other forms of display include distraction display, in which a bird attempts to lure a predator from its nest

Drumming An instrumental sound often made by vibrating the bill against a branch

Eruption A large-scale movement of birds from their breeding area, when numbers are high but food is short

Eye-ring A ring of colour around the eye

Eyestripe A stripe of colour running as a line through the eye

Family A category in classification, grouping genera that are closely related; also the family group of a pair (or single adult) with young

Feral Living wild, in a sustainable population, but derived from captive stock or from domestic stock that has escaped, or that has been introduced into an area where the species either does not naturally occur or, as in the case of the Feral Pigeon, from which it has disappeared as a truly wild bird

Genus A grouping of species (or, sometimes, a single species if the genus is "monotypic") that are closely related, recognized by the same first word in the scientific name; plural "genera"

Immature Not yet fully adult or able to breed; some species, such as larger gulls, have a sequence of changing immature plumages for three or four years, while others are unable to breed for several years but show no sign of such immaturity in their plumage pattern

Juvenile The plumage of a bird in its first flight, before its first moult

Moult The shedding of old feathers and growth of new replacements, in a systematic fashion that is characteristic of the species

Migrant A species that spends part of the year in one geographical area and part in another, "migrating" between the two

Order A category in classification, grouping families according to their presumed relationship

Pigeon's milk A cheesy secretion from the crop of pigeons, rich in protein and fat, which is fed to developing nestlings

Race A more or less distinct group within a species, defined by geographical area; also "subspecies"

Rare Found in very small numbers or low densities, or an individual bird found outside its normal range (a "rarity" or "vagrant")

Roost A place where birds sleep, or the act of sleeping. "A roost" infers a communal nature

Secure Of a population that is not currently or foreseeably threatened

Song A vocal performance with a pattern characteristic of the species; may attract a mate, or repel intruders from a territory

Song-flight A special and usually distinctive flight in which the song is performed

Species A group of living organisms, individuals of which can breed and produce fertile offspring, but which do not or cannot breed with individuals of other species

Streaked Marked with lines of colour aligned lengthwise along the body

Subspecies A more or less distinct group within a species, defined by geographical area; also "race"

Underwing The underside of the wing

Upperwing The upper surface of the wing

Vagrant An individual bird that has accidentally strayed outside its normal range; also a species that is only found in such circumstances in a given area, such as the Northern Parula, a "vagrant" in Europe

Wingpit The base of the underside of the wing, the "axillaries"

Wingbar A line of colour across the coverts on the closed wing or along the extended wing as a bar or stripe

Young An imprecise term to indicate an immature bird, from a nestling to a full grown bird in immature plumage

Index

Page numbers in **bold** refer to entries in the bird and plant profile sections; numbers in *italics* refer to illustrations.

Acknowledgments

Cobalt id would like to thank the following for their assistance with this book: Peter Holden for additional text and invaluable editorial guidance; Rob Hume for additional text, illustrations, and informed comment; Richard Bird for indexing; Richard Chappell, Ennis Jones, and John Ferguson for their enthusiastic help in the photography of their special gardens; Roger Crabb for illustrations of bird gardens and advice on wildlife gardening; all at FLPA for their help and guidance on image sources; Viking Optical; Trevor Codlin (digiscoping.co.uk); Christine Percy and all at Swarovski UK Ltd; and Rebecca Johns.

Commissioned photography: David Tipling, Peter Anderson
Commissioned illustration: John Plumer

Abbreviations key: t = top; b = bottom; l = left; r = right; c = centre. Pictures in columns are numbered top to bottom; pictures in rows are numbered left to right.

Ardea: 45c, 63tl2; Bill Coster Pictures Ltd 10tc; Bob Gibbons 42bl, 45br; Brian Bevan 34tr; Chris Knights 44cr1, 66br; Dennis Avon 53tl1; John Daniels 29b, 32tr, 80tr; M Watson 19b4; Steve Hopkin 39tr.

Bruce Coleman: Harald Lange 36tr.

Cobalt id: Marek Walisiewicz 9c.

Chris Gomersall: 18cr, 70b1, 70b2.

CJ Images: 16b4, 17b3, 20b3, 25b1, 26b8, 29tl2, 34bl; CJW 18b4; David White 5r5, 8, 16b1, 16b2, 17b2, 17b4, 17b5, 18b1, 18b5, 19b1, 19b2, 19b5, 20b1, 20b2, 20b4, 24b1, 24b4, 25b2, 25b3, 25b4, 26c, 31t1, 31t2, 31t3, 32bc, 33bc, 34bc, 35bl, 35b5, 36c, 60l1, 60l2, 60, 64l2, 64l4; M Read 34br; Outhouse 26b1, 26b2, 26b3, 26b4, 26b5, 26b6, 26b7.

FLPA: A Wharton 45tr; DT Grewcock 63r5; D Warren 35br; David Dalton 44bl; David Hosking 10br, 34l, 38bl, 66tl, 83cb, 90; E&D Hosking 30tr, 31cr; E Hosking 75bl; Foto Natura Stock 71b3; H Clark 67b2, 69cr; John Hawkins 33tr; R Wilmshurst 63r3, 63r4, 81l1; Ray Bird 11tr, 11t4; Richard Brooks 68cr; Robert Canis 30cr; Roger Tidman 38br, 67tl.

Garden Picture Library: Juliette Wade 42br; Lynne Brotchie 63; Sunniva Harte 60l3.

Garden World Images: 46bl.

Natural Visions: Brian Rogers 43c; Heather Angel 45bl, 48bl, 48br, 55tl, 59tl.

Mary Evans Picture Library: 7bl.

Mike Lane: 25cl.

Mike Read: 09br, 16b3, 17b1, 18b2, 28tr, 70b1, 70c, 81r.

NHPA: Eric Soder 16cl, 68bl; Joe Blossom 11; John Buckingham 22tr; Manfred Danegger 67b5; Paal Hermansen 44cr2; Stephen Dalton 4, 44tr, 67b1, 67b4; Susanne Danegger 39.

Oxford Scientific Films: Bob Gibbons 59br; Deni Bown 46tr, 58tl; Dennis Green/SAL 35tr; Lothar Lenz/Okapia 31br; Michael Leach 46br.

Roger Crabb: 47cl1.

RSPB: 30b, 32bl, 63r1; Bob Glover 15c, 32br; Chris Gomersall 16b5, 19tl; Chris Knights 67b3; Geoff Simpson 47cl2; George McCarthy 14b; Jan Halady 6c; Malcolm Hunt 10tl; Mark Hamblin 24l, 63r2, 71tr; Maurice Walker 71tr; Mike Richards 9tr; Ray Kennedy 28bl; Richard Brooks 88b2; Richard Revels 43tl; Robert Smith 85br; Steve Knell 64tl; Tony Hamblin 14tr.

Science Photo Library: Dr Kari Lounatmaa 29tl1.

Windrush Photos: 19r, 68t; David Tipling 2, 5r3, 5r4, 18b3, 19b3, 25t, 33bl, 60, 78; F Desmette 70b3; G Langsbury 6bl; George McCarthy 66bl1; Gordon Langsbur 33c; J Hollis 1b; Roger Tidman 66bl2; Tom Ennis 20c.

Every effort has been made to trace the copyright holders. The publisher apologizes for any unintentional omissions and would be pleased, in such cases, to place an acknowledgment in future editions of this book.

All other images © Dorling Kindersley
For further information see: www.dkimages.com